DON'T THEY KNOW THE WORLD STOPPED BREATHING?

**Reminiscences of a French Child
During the Holocaust Years**

by Renée Fersen-Osten

SHAPOLSKY PUBLISHERS, NEW YORK

Where is the train taking us now?

Through the glass window the beautiful countryside seems untouched. The cows graze peacefully, as though nothing had happened, their big bulging eyes stare at us as we pass by.

"Don't they know the world stopped breathing?"

Spring is almost in the air. The red, white and blue wild flowers start to push the ground, along the way, wherever a piece of uncultivated earth welcomes them.

The *marguerites*, the *bleuets*, and the *coquelicots*. Our national country flowers. The colors of our flag. The subject of so many songs and poems. The inspiration of our most famous painters.

"Don't they know the world stopped breathing?"

Next to us, other passengers are laughing, cutting big chunks of light brown bread and fragrant salamis full of garlic. They are opening bottles of deep red wine. *A votre santé! A votre santé!* They toast, hitting their glasses against each other with loud clicking sounds.

"Don't they know the world stopped breathing?"

DEDICACE

I dedicate this book to:

My gallant and courageous parents, Annette and Maurice.

My sister Yvonne, who held my hand, who cut my hair, who did not cry.

Oma. Thank you for your guiding hand, for having shared your life with us. You represent the Omas so many will never have the joy of knowing.

My husband Bernard, who comforts me when the shadows once more creep in to engulf my spirit.

My precious children, Marc and Caren, and the children they will someday have. Through them I fully understood the magnitude of the cruelty, the desperation of our Holocaust.

May they have nothing but peace and serenity. May they never know what we had to learn: the survival of condemned innocents.

All of you, who never had a chance.

Table of Contents

SUNDAYS
ARE
SO
SPECIAL!

H*ope,*
is a slice
of sunshine.

Hope,
is a breath
of air.

Hope,
is a leaf
on a tree.

Hope,
is when all else
is lost.

The place is called Toulouse. A city in the south of France. Some days the sun shone in Toulouse. Some days it rained. I don't really mean the weather, you know. I mean how you feel in your heart, deep in your heart.

My jail is surrounded by the confining walls of the convent where I live, and do not love, or feel warm, or feel happy. I am here in hiding. I am a Jew child. A Catholic convert. A floating orphan. I mean, not here, not there. If I was a true orphan, I would know where I belong, but I know I have parents, maybe?

Hope must never be lost. Oh God! if you exist, let me laugh, let me be a child, even your child. If you are so loving, can't you caress me sometimes? I need to know you're here. This, is not what I need. This, is not what I want.

Breakfast will come soon. A metal bowl, a metal spoon, a hard piece of bread, a hot ladle of coffee. After the benediction you may start this feast. Your black uniform has a self-belted sash, that you tie in a bow around your skinny waist. Ah! If the sash were red, or green, or blue? Would you then think God really loves you?

The work never seems to end. If it's Monday to Saturday, you know what you must do. There is much studying going on. There's also potato peeling, and learning to embroider, pulling threads to make neat little rows of perfect little holes. Your fingers hurt when you pull, thread after thread, endlessly. You must count every stitch, and your eyes tear sometimes.

The prayer is important. You march under the arches toward the chapel. You ache, but no one knows. Your stomach feels empty. A void fills it. It seems larger and larger. You enter the church, single file, kneel, bend your head, recite well-worn prayers, praising things you don't understand, or know, things that have no faces, and no smiles.

The pain is always there. Your knees ache, from the hard bench beneath. You'd like to look up, giggle, be mischievous, all of which are crimes, punishable on confession Saturday. "You will recite, for absolution, five Ave Marias, two Ave Marias, one Ave Maria."

The best day is what I wait for. Monday to Saturday are the same. But, once a week, comes Sunday — and that is always special.

Sunday, you may wear a dress.
Sunday, you get communion,
if you're free of sins, of course.
Sunday, breakfast has jam and a roll.
Sunday, you run in the yard.
Sunday, you can talk to a friend,
planning, plotting, dreaming.
And, well,
Sunday,
I take out the picture!

I keep the picture in a small flat metal box, hidden under the mattress of my bed, right on the pillow side. This way, I can say good night before I fall asleep, and take them along when I dream.

When I dream that I'll wake up, and they'll all be here, like before.

When I dream I am in the picture, and they are surrounding me, and I feel happy, and I smile.

I keep the picture wrapped in a little white handkerchief that was Maman's. It has lace all around and, in one corner, is an embroidered flower. The handkerchief is a little dirty now, but I don't care. I'll never ever wash it. It smells of the perfume Maman used to wear and, when I take it out, I feel she is here with me. I always hold it against my cheek before I open the picture to breathe some of the scent.

Every time I look at the picture I feel like crying. I try not to. I don't want anyone to see me and ask questions. I want to be alone with the picture.

So I can talk to them.

So I can make secret wishes.

So I can make believe I am in the picture once more, sitting on the high round wooden stool, between Papa and Maman. Papa has his hand on my shoulder, and Maman's fingers are around mine, holding on to my pinky. I still feel the little gold ring they gave me for my birthday. I could see it shining bright in the picture, even though it was as small as a little bird's eye. When they gave it to me they said it was still too big for a little five year old girl like me!

The ring had a tiny red stone.

"It's a garnet! Your birthstone!" they had told me proudly as I admired it. The ring had made me feel all grown up. I'd be starting in the big school next year. I wouldn't have to nap at midday anymore, like a baby.

I touch my finger now and feel the emptiness of my bare skin. The ring is gone. Papa is gone. Maman is gone. Oma too. Only Yvonne, my big sister is left. Every day I pray they wouldn't take her. It is my biggest fear.

Yes, Sundays are so special. It's my favorite time with them. Papa thinks so too. It's the day we can have a conversation, and I tell him all the big things that happened to me during the week. For Maman, I keep the more private ones. The ones I am not so sure Papa would understand.

I always start with a kiss, by brushing my lips on their faces, making sure not to wet it and ruin the shiny surface of the photograph. It's the only picture I have. I don't want to do anything to spoil it. It's black and white, but I see it in full color.

Papa always smiles at me in the picture. Papa was so beautiful. His deep, large, dark brown eyes told you right away how he felt. You knew if he was happy, or sad, just by looking into them. His narrow oval face was like a frame around the straight nose, the pink mouth, full and round, with two pointy arches on the upper lip. His skin had an olive complexion. They always said: "Little Renée has her father's color." And I was so proud, as though it was a special legacy!

Papa's hair was full, curly, black with some silver shining through, here and there. He smelled good, of woods and trees. I loved sitting on his lap and putting my head in his neck. It felt safe and warm, and wonderful. Even his name, Maurice, sounded as though it belonged only to him, and to no one else.

Maman was quite the opposite. Her pink skin, blond hair and bright blue eyes contrasted all his features. When you saw them standing together, it was as if an artist had painted his canvas with all the brilliant colors of the rainbow. One could not do without the other. They blended like the sunshine and the earth and the trees, giving you all you needed to fill your eyes and your heart with the joy of beauty.

Maman's name, Annette, seemed to dance as Papa called it out so loud and clear. Maman favored pretty flower printed dresses and she wore big wide-brimmed hats to enhance and shade her fair complexion. She loved to sing, and often some sweet melody would accompany me as I drifted into sleep.

"Maman, come today. I need you so! It's cold here. I'm frightened. It's only been two birthdays since the picture. Soon, maybe I won't remember all the little things you were to me. Don't let more birthdays go by. Maman, I'm waiting. Please come back and take me away!"

I know it's foolish to ask the picture for a miracle to happen, but I ask anyway. They might hear me somehow. And, if they do, they'll listen. I know how much they love me. They want to be here. I am sure.

Oma is in the picture too. Oma, my beloved Grandmother. She stands near Papa in the photograph. She belongs to him. The heart of my heart, she always called him. I've never known life without Oma, until now. Oma is as tall as Papa. Her face looks just like his, but wrinkled and parched like after a storm.

Her hair is arranged in a silver halo standing all around. She lets it puff out like a crown and ties the ends into a tight bun, which she fastens in the back on the top of her head with long silver pins that have little waves in them to stop them from falling out.

Oma always wore plain dresses, not like Maman's fancy ones. She used only flat shoes, and didn't seem to care if she was pretty, although I always thought she was so beautiful — especially her hands, which were square and gnarled, with big blue veins and nubby bones that made some of her fingers crooked. I loved them so.

Oma kept her hands doing things all the time, knitting, crocheting, cooking, baking, fixing things here and there. She only stopped three times a day. She'd sit in her favorite chair, remove the little silver rectangular box from her apron pocket. In it were three pieces of a cigarette. Every morning, Oma took one out of a pack she kept near her bed and carefully cut it into three parts with a small scissor. She placed them in the silver container, in which she also kept the small black cigarette holder.

When it was time to rest, Oma would place one piece of the cigarette in the holder, light it with a long wooden kitchen match, and sit quietly smoking until the little red circle became whitish ash at the end of the holder.

Oma picked me up at school every day and then, once home, we'd do things together until the others arrived. We'd bake bread, or shell peas, or plant flowers, and she'd always wait until I was finished with my portion until she showed me the next thing we were going to do together.

"Oma, what I learn now, is not how to expect the sweet challah to rise in the oven while we anxiously wait to open the door and remove the golden treasure!

Oma, what I learn now, is not to love what I must do, for your hand is not holding mine, showing me the way.

Oma, I miss you so, every day, every day. Please let me see you again, my Oma. Please wait for me!"

Then in the picture is Yvonne, my big sister. She holds Papa's hand. He called her "my first violin" and they made music together.

Yvonne is five years older than I. I always had to look way up when I spoke to her, because she was tall for a ten-year-old, and I was short for my age. Yvonne was always my idol. She also frightened me because she wanted me to know, at all times, that she was in control and that I must listen and do as she said.

That was all I wanted anyway, and even though it hurt some-times, I wouldn't dream of saying no. Like that time when she told me to climb up and up and up on that tall wall bordering a house. Then she said: "Jump!" and I did. She said I'd be like an airplane and would fly in the air. Well, I believed it. Maman was so mad when they had to take me to the hospital with some broken bones, but I didn't care. I would do it again if she told me to.

Yvonne is so pretty. Her eyes are like Papa's, but in a greenish color. Her face is round like Maman's. Her brown hair, in the picture, was cut below the neck, curving gently with a center part and heavy straight bangs in front.

She didn't want me around when her friends were there. But when she was alone she'd let me follow her and, some-times, she'd let me be someone in a game — like the dog, or the maid, or even the baby on occasion.

We didn't play games anymore now. I got to see Yvonne once a week on Sunday for a long visit, and every day for a few minutes if we passed each other in the covered halls on our way to the chapel or to a classroom.

The smaller children were in a separate wing of the convent, and we rarely had occasion to be together in any activity. Sometimes Yvonne was in charge of serving breakfast with another girl. When she did, she always gave me a little extra *café au lait* when she ladled it into my metal bowl. I know she also picked out a bigger piece of bread, quickly dropping it as she moved on the line, so it wouldn't look as though she was favoring me.

I couldn't live without her. They tried once to separate us, sending the smaller children to another convent. The nuns know what I'll do if they take her away. They saw that the last time. I hope they don't try it again. She's all I have. No one can take her from me. She's my life now.

Sometimes I look at myself in the picture. A small skinny girl. My face is long and oval like Papa's and I am dark as he is. My hair is very black and braided with large ribbons tied in bows at each end. Maman loved to put huge bows on me. Sometimes on top of my head, sometimes in the back. She always took much time to lovingly brush and fix my long black hair. I would sit patiently and let her.

I hardly recognize myself in the picture anymore. It seems so long ago. The pretty dress is gone. The white shiny patent leather shoes are gone. The smile is gone. The bows are gone. My long beautiful black hair is gone. Only the picture is left.

Soon, will come Monday.
And then Tuesday,
and then Wednesday,
and then Thursday,
and then Friday,

and then Saturday,
and then,
it will be Sunday.
And Sundays are so special!
And Sunday I'll take the picture out!
"Goodbye till then."

I wrap the photograph in the scented handkerchief and it will
wait in the little metal box, and I think silently.

And once,
there was a garden,
and a child,
and a tree.

And once,
there was a father,
and a mother,
and a dog.

And once,
there was a house,
and a sister,
and a grandma.

And once,
there was life.

PAPA

HAS

A

UNIFORM

WITH

SHINY

BRASS

BUTTONS

I look for the shade under the old oak tree that is in the corner of the courtyard.

Sisters Marie-Joseph and Marie-Paule are organizing a ball game at the opposite end. They formed two teams, and everyone is busy deciding which side they want to play on. I said I wasn't feeling well, so I didn't have to join.

What a beautiful Sunday it is today. The sun is shining and I promised I would take them outside as soon as the weather got nice. I feel them through the pocket of my cardigan sweater, the one my Godmother Nanita knitted for me and sent to the convent for Christmas. They are safe in the handkerchief in my pocket. I won't let the picture get wrinkled. I am very careful not to hurt them.

The teams are formed now, and the girls start to play ball. The rest of the courtyard is empty, and they won't see me if I snuggle against the old oak tree and take the picture out. I put the sweater on the ground and settle comfortably with my knees clutched together half-way up. No one's around. Carefully, I reach into the pocket of the sweater laying on the soft grass. The handkerchief got a little humid from the dew. I must watch it next time.

First, I caress my cheek against it, as I usually do.

"Bonjour Papa, Maman, Oma. I promised, remember, I'd take you out on the first Sunday of good spring weather. Breathe and look around. See, the flowers are starting to bloom in their beds, and the trees have fresh new leaves! See, the sky is blue. It is all so pretty.

Today, under the tree, I feel almost like it was long ago. Remember when we were together, in the little house.

I didn't know how much I loved you then!

The year is 1940. The house is in St. Gratien, a small village about twenty kilometers from Paris. We lived there before the war broke out.

We were a family then — Papa, Maman, Oma, Yvonne, Mirka,

our German shepherd dog, and me. I was the little one.

I went to a tiny nursery school where the activity was mostly playing, taking a rest on little cots at noontime, and more playing until it was time to go home.

Mirka was tall and strong. She would take me to school in the morning. I held on to her collar and off we went. She was taller than I, but she knew my walking pace and slowed down to keep in step with me.

When we arrived at the school I would kiss her on the cheek, give her a hug, and say goodbye. She would watch a bit sadly as I entered the red painted door.

"Goodbye, Mirka. Go home. Come on, go home." I would say. She'd slowly turn, wagging her tail between her legs, seeming to mutter: "Oh, why must I leave? I want to go to school too."

At two o'clock she came back to get me, much more happy this time. Oma also came to pick me up. Sometimes she was late, and I would stand on the front steps anxiously waiting. From afar she would wave the little paper bag, showing me she had it.

"It" was the *petit pain au chocolat* I loved so. Oma stopped at the bakery and got me a fresh one every day, right out of the oven. Sometimes the baker was late and she would nervously wait for them to be ready, hesitating between being on time to pick me up or coming empty-handed.

The house in St. Gratien was located on the corner of a quiet and sunny street, very similar to all others that made up the small suburban village on the outskirts of Paris. It was surrounded by a lovely garden enclosed by a fence.

As you entered through the gate in front, Mirka's house imposingly faced you on the right. Nobody passed who did not belong. Mirka was absolute master of the place. She once ripped the pants off a mailman who was replacing the one who came daily. Poor Papa had to go to court and pay a big fine. But, Mirka loved us and protected us, and so she could do no wrong.

There was a big old tree in our garden. It had a huge trunk and lots of branches that you could climb on, and that shielded you if you wanted to hide. A little corner of the garden was assigned to me. There, I could dig, plant things, water them and watch them grow.

One day, Papa put on a khaki-colored suit with shiny brass buttons, high leather boots and a funny-looking hat. I had never seen them before. I was bewildered by the uniform. Today, he looked very sad. "Why are you not happy today Papa?" I asked.

Maman also looked different. The air was strange all around. Even Mirka wasn't talking. When Papa lifted me in the air and hugged me, it was so tight I felt my bones cracking. He kissed me and whispered:

"I'll be back. I'll be back soon."

"Back? Where are you going Papa? Aren't you going to be here in the morning to give me my *café au lait* and butter my baguette before Mirka takes me to school?"

"No. Not tomorrow, little one, not tomorrow." he said sadly.

Days went by. Something had changed. Maman drove the car now, and she was all alone when she left for work in the morning. I could feel the sadness all around. Oma sometimes forgot my *petit pain au chocolat* when she picked me up. She would sit at the window, hours and hours, looking out. Waiting, waiting for Papa to come home.

The big people always listened to the talk on the radio now. Before, we used to listen to music, but nobody liked music anymore. All the neighbors talked outside on the street when they met on the way to the baker or to get milk. Everyone was asking: "What will happen now? What will happen next?"

My garden looked the same, so I spent hours digging and talking to the flowers I had grown there. They didn't care about the radio. Only they talked to me now. The adults had no patience for a little girl who didn't understand anything.

Mirka also didn't care about the radio. So, my company was Big Tree, Tiny Garden and my loving dog. I spent most of my time with them now.

Often, I would climb up on the first lush branch of Big Tree.

Mirka stretched out on the ground below. No one could see you among the leaves. You could talk loud and dream silently and not care about the radio.

"Mirka, someday you and I will go on a long, long expedition together," I'd tell her. " Not just to school, but far, far away." I'd clarify to make sure she understood. "They'll let us when I get a little bigger, you'll see. If they don't we'll go anyway. We'll see the lions and the tigers. Like the pictures in my school book. I think they speak another language there, but don't worry," I reassured her. "I'll talk for you and you'll watch over me. We'll manage, you'll see Mirka!" And then I went on addressing Big Tree. "You watch. Soon I'll be able to climb to your next branch. I want to go higher because then my legs won't hang down and be seen from below. You know, if I can reach the next branch, I'll be able to put my feet on this one. Then, we'll be all alone. No one will know we are together up here. Well, no one except Mirka," I quickly added in case she had heard me.

"You know she also doesn't care about the radio, so it's all right if she knows about us. I wish you'd let me live with you all the time Big Tree. I feel so cozy here."

One day everyone got so happy. We cooked a big dinner. We set a big table. Papa, Papa is coming home!

It was good to have him back. Now Maman was happy. Now Oma didn't sit at the window, staring into space. Now they talked to me again. They had time. They didn't listen to the radio. Papa wore his normal clothes. He threw the wood stick at Mirka. She ran around the yard before returning it. Mirka was happy too.

A few days later I saw Papa wearing the khaki uniform with the shiny brass buttons, the boots, the funny hat.

"No, Papa. No. Don't put this on," I said. "I don't want you to go. Never, never. I won't let you go. I know I am the smallest here and can only reach up to your knee, but I know how to stop you — and I will."

Maman, Oma and my sister were standing sadly around Papa

saying goodbye. I knew what to do to stop him. I had found the way. The only way. I ran to Big Tree. Climbed up the first branch.

"Big Tree, hide me. Hide me." I cried out. "He won't leave if he can't find me. He can't leave without my goodbye." I said. "My legs are showing Big Tree. They'll find me and pull me down. I cannot wait until I am bigger. I'll have to climb to your higher branches now. I know it's too high for me Big Tree, but I must do it. I have no choice."

My heart beating fast I climbed and climbed, not looking down, but only up. I heard his voice searching for me.

"My little one. My little one. Come and kiss your Papa. I must go now. Come and kiss me goodbye," Papa called out.

You'll never find me. I thought. You'll never get me down. You cannot leave without kissing me goodbye. You won't be able to. You won't leave! I knew I had found the only thing that could stop him. It was simple.

Repeatedly he called out to me. Then Maman did, insisting, commanding.

I would never come down. Couldn't they see he wouldn't leave without my goodbye? Couldn't they see I was doing it for all of them? Didn't they want Papa to stay? Why were they calling me?

Silence. Deep silence followed. Everyone went back in the house. I won! I did it!

It was getting dark. Big Tree told me it was time to go home. I had never been so high before and suddenly realized I would not be able to come down alone. Maybe Papa could get me, now that he didn't leave? I waited, but no one came. Mirka kept circling around and around Big Tree.

"Come down, little one. If you can't jump. I will catch you on my back. Come on. I won't let you get hurt," she said.

I walked into the house. Triumphant. Joyous.

Oma was sitting at the window, staring into space.

Maman and my sister were at the radio, listening to the voices.

No one was talking to me anymore.

He had left. Left. Without my goodbye.

I had lost all my powers, and nothing mattered any more.

It seemed as if nothing would ever be right anymore. Soon the radio told everyone to go away. Not just Papa, but all of us.

"Leave your homes!" they said. "Go to free France!" they said.

Free France? What is Free France? Didn't we already live there?

Maman said we would have to leave for Free France.

No. No. How will Papa find us? "Papa won't know where Free France is, when he comes home and doesn't find us," I said.

Mirka wasn't going to Free France with us. Maman said there was no room in the car. There would not be enough food or water. We had to leave Mirka behind. It seemed no one wanted Mirka. Some neighbors were leaving also. Others said there was no food to feed another mouth.

One day, the neighbor came to the house. He tied Mirka to Big Tree. He took something black from his bag. He pointed it at Mirka. It made a big noise, and Mirka fell on the ground.

She had blood all over. Her eyes were closed. She was motionless. Now, everyone started digging a large hole under Big Tree. They gave me a shovel too.

They put Mirka in the hole and covered her with earth. Then we all stood around and Maman said we should say goodbye to Mirka. Mirka would stay home, she said, under Big Tree, and she would sleep peacefully forever and ever.

I stood there, feeling completely lost.

First, Papa left.

Now, Mirka would sleep forever under Big Tree.

How would I go to school without Mirka?

I didn't want her to sleep when I climbed Big Tree. I wanted her to bark and circle when it was time to go home. I wanted her to talk to us. The three of us belonged together.

She couldn't sleep forever and ever. I wanted her to wake up sometimes. We had plans, Mirka and I. Soon, we were going to leave, to see the lions and the tigers, in a far away land. They spoke another language there. I would translate for her, and she would watch over me.

"Mirka, please..." I implored. "Wake up sometime! Please Mirka! Don't sleep forever and ever!"

And then with despair, I addressed Big Tree.

"Big Tree, I know you go under the ground. They told me you have roots that reach way down below under the earth. Ask one of your roots to hold Mirka tight and keep her warm. It must be cold down there. Then, when she wants to wake up and join us, your root can shake the earth to wake her, and she can come up to be with us again! Big Tree, you've always helped me. Please don't let Mirka sleep forever and ever!" I insisted.

Maman, Oma and my sister started packing. They put pots, pans and dishes in boxes. They stripped my bed and put the mattress on the roof of the car and tied it up with rope. They took clothes out of the armoire and put them in the car too. Then they said:

"Come on. Come on little one. We're leaving now!"

"Leaving? Leaving? Where? Why? I don't want to leave. Maman. please. Why must we go?" I cried.

And Maman said: "You don't understand. Just take a toy and come. Don't ask questions. You don't understand."

"I don't understand? What don't I understand? That I won't wait for Mirka and Oma and my little *pain au chocolat* at school anymore? That the flowers in my garden will not get water and be talked to anymore? That Big Tree will cry of loneliness everyday, because I don't climb its branches anymore? That Mirka will not wake up if I am not here to make it happen with Big Tree. That she and I won't leave together far, far away anymore? That you have destroyed my bed, and threw the mattress on top of the car, so that I shall never, never cuddle up and sleep there anymore? That Papa doesn't know where Free France is and will never find us anymore? Everything is gone. Everything will sleep forever now.

You don't understand. You don't understand!" I shouted.

We all squeezed into the car. Maman, Oma, my sister,

Grandma and Grandpa from Paris, and some other people I didn't know. Some were standing on the little steps at the outside of the doors on each side of the car.

I looked back and saw the house get smaller and smaller. It just didn't seem possible that we were leaving.

I did not remember ever going away anywhere far.

What was far like?

Far was not where Mirka and I were going to go.

Far was leaving everything you loved behind knowing, even if you were the little one who didn't really understand, that things would never, ever be the same again.

Hope,
is a slice
of sunshine.

Hope,
is a breath
of air.

Hope,
is a leaf
on a tree.

Hope,
is when all else
is lost.

3

FREE
FRANCE
IS
ON
THE
OTHER
SIDE

T*hey fled*
their lives.
They fled
their homes.

It was better,
elsewhere
they heard.
It was safer,
elsewhere
they thought.

Day and night
and
night and day.

They carried
their burdens.
They carried
their children.

And then,
they could go
no more,
for the gates
only opened
to the few.

Thursday we get a history lesson. Sister Marie-Catherine comes to our classroom to instruct us.

I like Sister Marie-Catherine. She is young and not as strict as some of the other Sisters. She is pretty too. You can only see her eyes, nose and mouth, because the large white coif covers all her head and hugs the contours of her face all around. I wonder if she has hair underneath the coif. Some girls say the Sisters shave their hair completely. Others say they keep some, especially if they are young. I guess I'll never know.

I like history. I always look forward to Sister Marie-Catherine's lesson. Today, we are going to hear about Napoleon Bonaparte and the battle of Waterloo. I think Napoleon Bonaparte is exciting. All the things he did are so big. Yet, in many ways, I feel he was sad and wanted to do some good. He had a lot of dreams, but he didn't know how to achieve them. I feel sorry for him, sometimes. I wish I would have known him in person.

I am not always attentive in class. Often the Sisters reprimand me for this. My mind wanders all the time. I find it difficult not to think of several things at once.

Today, as Sister Marie-Catherine talked of the battle of Waterloo and the cannons and all the soldiers, I started to remember Maman. Maman was a soldier too. No, Maman was a General, just like Napoleon, even bigger, I think.

Maman had more courage than anyone I knew, or had heard about, in all the history lessons. Maman had fought the biggest battle, and I had been there to see it.

I will never forget that day.

Whenever I think about it I feel frightened, just like when it happened, and then, I am so proud because of what she did. Some day, I will put her in the history books, right near Napoleon. I want all the children to know what happened that day, and I shall call it: *"The Day General Annette Fersen Conquered the World!"* To me, it was the world. I wouldn't be here if not for what she did.

Sister Marie-Catherine is speaking. I hear her soft voice, but my head goes to that day. That day when we all had to run from the house in St. Gratien, and leave everything behind, and Papa was away somewhere fighting, and Maman had to drive the car, and Mirka had to stay home sleeping under Big Tree.

Yes, that trip would always stay with me. We were running, and still they caught us, and still we didn't escape.

The cars on the road were bumper to bumper. Many people walked. Some were on bicycles. The cars were full with people and things you needed when you stopped at night. Mattresses, pots, blankets, some food and water.

The people on foot would mount the side steps of the car, sometimes, to get a bit of rest but still keep moving.

It was called the EXODUS — the French of the north moving toward the south, which was not yet occupied by the Germans in 1940. They fled in the hope they would escape the occupation and find refuge in the south.

Not everyone could go. You needed special permission and passage papers from the authorities, but many people did not want to wait for official permission. They just left.

I remember the heat, being very crowded inside the car. I remember Maman driving, stopping all the time, squeezed between the thousands of cars in front and in back of us. Many people were on foot, carrying bags on their backs. Many were dragging little children by the hand. Some were carrying them on their backs. I remember feeling sad, sad because they had to walk.

At night Maman stopped the car altogether. The rope that held the mattress on top of the roof was removed and the mattress was laid out on the side of the street.

"Lie down. Lie down and sleep a while," she would say.

We would sleep a little, and then it would be someone else's turn to lie down on the mattress.

Maman would put tiny pieces of wood on some stones. She then put the pot on it and threw some things in a little water. It tasted nice, but I don't remember what it was. Just something warm that made you feel happy for a short while.

There were big army trucks all around, with lots of soldiers dressed in khaki uniforms like Papa's. I remember one day I got very very sick and burning. Scarlet fever they said it was. Maman kept going from truck to truck begging for a little water. She said her child was burning. She said her child was dying. She said she needed water for her child.

Oh, I felt so bad for Maman. Poor Maman, who had to beg, beg, for her dying child.

The nights and days never ended.
Where was Free France anyway?
Was there such a thing?
Whispers started humming one day.
Free France is on the other side, the other side.
It was on the other side? No more begging?
No more mattresses on the street,
where you took your sleeping turn?
Maybe Free France would be St. Gratien?
Maybe Papa was waiting on the other side?
Maybe Mirka was also waiting?
Maybe Free France was pink, and blue and green!
Not gray and brown and black!

We arrived at the border that separated the country in half. It was nightfall. The sky was full of clouds. They looked mean, menacing. Looking down at us with all the power they had. They, big and strong, up in the sky. And we, so little, so tired, hugging the earth, crawling the ground like bugs.

The border was full of soldiers holding enormous rifles. There were gates closing off the entire area, making it impossible to drive through. The soldiers stopped everyone. You had to show them a Paper. A Paper that said you could either go to Free France or could not. The paper decided. If you could not, you had to turn and go back. The gates only opened for the ones who could.

When we came to the gate we waited anxiously, wondering what would happen to us. The soldier looked into the car.

"Good evening Madame. May I see your permit papers,

please?" he asked.

"Sure Officer, sure Officer," Maman said, as she started looking into her bag feverishly. "Uh, uh, Officer, please..." she muttered. "Could I pull over there, on the side, and get all these documents out for you?"

"Certainly Madame. Just go here to the left and get your things together, then turn and come back to the gate when you are ready," he replied.

Maman started the engine. She turned slowly to the left and, suddenly, she made a full turn, back to the gate, full speed, crashing through it like a bullet.

Passing the soldiers,
the shotguns,
the lights,
the signs,
Going...going...speeding...speeding...

"Halt! Stop! Halt! Stop!" they screamed, and then, "Shoot! Fire! Shoot! Fire!"

Soldiers ran out from the barracks to the left and right of the barricades. They lined up all along and started shooting their rifles, as they had been ordered to do. There was much panic. Huge lights were beamed in our direction.

Commands,
Screams,
Sirens,
Lights,
all following us without pity.

Maman went like the speed of lightning, never looking back, not even at us, as the bullets were fired all around, hissing and burning.

"Heads Down!" Maman screamed. "Heads Down!"

Maman, Maman, we're here I thought.

We're closing our eyes, our ears, holding our heads.

We're scared. Where are you taking us Maman?

Is this Free France?

Everything was shaking and rattling inside and outside the car. It was dark and scary down there on the floor, and the lights were shooting up like lightning in the sky.

"Stay Down! Stay Down!" she commanded. "They can't follow us here. They can't. If they don't get us with the guns we'll be free. Free — in Free France."

The noises grew further and further away. Total darkness followed the lightning. Total silence.

Maman stopped the car. Everyone looked at each other. She counted us.

Were we all here? Were we all in one piece?

Did someone get blown up in the flight?

Were we all alive?

Maman looked so pale and tired. She had performed a miracle. She had ignored the uniforms, the guns, the lights, the shots. Her courage, her fierce will, had defeated all of them!

All of them who thought they were strong and powerful!

All of them who thought a paper was your destiny!

All of them who never thought one fearless woman, with a car full of small children, old people, pots and pans hanging on the side of the car, a mattress on the roof, would dare, dare pass — pass over them, risking death for all, to reach her destination and, eventually, all of our destinies.

Later on I made up this poem for Maman, in my head. I memorized it. I was going to save it for her birthday, and for when Papa found us. I still remember it.

"Maman, this is the poem. Please be there, somewhere."

TO MY MAMAN WHO CAN FLY OVER MOUNTAINS
WITHOUT WINGS, WHO HAS COURAGE,
WHO IS FEARLESS, WHO RISKS ALL.
I LOVE YOU MAMAN.

It seems to me,
you had no fear,

even though,
the end was near.

The soldiers were shooting,
the lights were blinding.
The voices were shrieking.
You did not hear.

The sky was heavy,
with approaching night.
The clouds hung low,
to show their might.

Your children
were frightened.
the old people too.
But you did not stop,
what you had to do.

I never recited the poem to her. We never celebrated birthdays anymore. It seemed so foolish when such bad things were happening to everyone.

I am sorry now. I wish I had told Maman the poem. So she would know how proud I was, and maybe she would remember it wherever she is now, and it would make her feel happy.

The long trip all the way down to the finish line was endless. When we reached the border of Spain we had to stop. The huge Pyrénées mountains, tall and imposing, faced us. They seemed to imply: "You shall go no further!"

The other side was Spain, presumably some other place where we were not wanted. The small village of Cardesse near Oloron-Ste.-Marie, deep in the valley, was the last stop.

Maman disposed of the car. There was no further place to go, no gasoline and, anyway, it was practically wrecked from the long journey. The bit of money she got for it would feed us for a while, seemingly the most important thing on her mind right now.

I vaguely remember a huge house full of people where we occupied a room. There was a long narrow road in front of the house, stretching out forever. I would sit at the window, looking down the stretch for hours.

Was I waiting for something to happen?

Was I waiting for someone to arrive?

Small children are like animals. Our sense of smell is sharp and we seem to know what will happen before it does. I don't know how long it took but, one day, during my hours of vigil, I saw a tiny figure of a person at the end of the long narrow road that stretched in a straight line forever. I knew, I smelled, I screamed:

"Maman, Maman, look it's Papa, it's Papa! He found us, he found us in Free France!"

She looked at me sadly. Why did I pursue the impossible? Always dreaming. Did I really think life would always comply according to my burning wishes?

I did not care. I knew. I started running, like a bird in flight, faster, faster. What I had been waiting for, all the way back when hiding in Big Tree, was happening now.

He had found us!

He could never have left forever!

He had not kissed me goodbye.

Breathlessly, I started to see the reality of his features. The khaki uniform, with the shiny brass buttons — old, worn, dirty. His boots full of mud, a small backpack strapped around his shoulders, his beautiful face emaciated, his great velvet eyes shining with expectation, relief and happiness.

He dropped the backpack, stopped moving, waiting for his "little one" to jump into his arms. He closed his arms around me, without words, just holding tight, rocking from one side to the other.

I forgave him now!

He had left without my kiss, without my goodbye, but I forgave him now. He wouldn't, he couldn't, ever, ever, be taken from my life again. My weapons, if needed, would be stronger. What I thought was foolproof, did not have enough power. I could see that now. But I forgave him, forgave him fully, and would never let him go.

They all came running down the road now, screaming with joy and happiness. He put me down to receive them. They were crying, hugging. Now they believed what I was waiting for was true. What I always knew would happen. He had to return. I had not kissed him goodbye.

The insistent tap on my shoulder, administered by the girl sitting next to me, was accompanied by Sister Marie-Catherine's voice in a loud pitch I wasn't accustomed to.

"Mademoiselle." Sister Marie-Catherine demanded, pointing her ruler at me. "Who won the battle of Waterloo?"

"Maman, Sister Marie-Catherine." I answered. "Maman won the battle of Waterloo!"

"What?" Sister Marie-Catherine asked.

I heard the others around me giggling. I suddenly realized what I had said and felt so foolish.

"You get the answer from the study book, and give me ten pages with the answer written on each line, for next Thursday!" she ordered.

"Yes, Sister Marie-Catherine," I sheepishly replied.

Did she know it was my Maman who won the battle? She'd know some day. Some day, when I'd put Maman in the history book, right next to Napoleon, everyone, everyone in the world would finally know the truth.

4

HEADS
AND
FEET
GO
TOGETHER

Sister Marie-Bernadette has deep black eyes and a dark complexion. She teaches Latin. She has a strong accent and sometimes I don't understand some words she uses.

Of course Latin is very boring, but we must learn it the Sisters say. It's supposed to be the root of our French language. They say no one speaks it anymore, so it is strange we must study it, but there is no choice.

The other day, Sister Marie-Bernadette compared some words in French, Italian and Spanish, showing us how they all had the same root from the Latin one. Then she told us how she had learned French easily because Spanish, her native language, also had the same Latin roots.

Someone asked Sister Marie-Bernadette why she had left Spain to come to live in France. She said her family had to leave because of political reasons. She explained Spain was not a free country, and that it was ruled by one man who did not give freedom to the people.

That's funny! I thought. I'd heard Spain was free and France was not. I'd heard it would be good to go there to hide, that there were no Germans in Spain!

"Please tell me then," I asked. "Why did many families try to go to Spain from France to run away from the Germans, and yet, you came here to run away from Spain? My family wanted to escape to Spain too."

Everyone turned to look at me, wondering why we would want to go to Spain when we were French. I became very red in the face. I realized what a terrible mistake I made and I almost started to cry.

"You must never, never tell anyone you are Jewish and what happened to your family," Mother Superior had insisted when she first admitted us into the convent.

Père Agathange, the Franciscan Monk Papa had befriended, was the one who had arranged for the convent to take us in. This way we would be safe from the Germans and no one would know we were Jewish. We'd have to become Catholics, he'd explained to Papa and Maman, so no one would suspect anything.

Why did I have to pretend anything? I had wondered. I never knew that I was something special or different before! All my friends in school were the same as I. Why did I have to hide now? It was very confusing, but I was told to listen and I tried very hard to keep all my secrets.

Only with Yvonne could I say things about the past. Even she would look around when we talked and tell me to keep my voice low so no one could hear us. Well, at least I could talk to them in the picture. I did it in my head, so there was no chance anyone could hear.

"Why did your family want to go to Spain?" Sister Marie-Bernadette asked me.

"I just invented it. I am sorry Sister," I said. I was stuttering and very embarrassed. It was a sin to make up untrue stories. "I'll confess on Saturday and will say an extra prayer to ask forgiveness, Sister."

Yvonne would be mad at me if she heard. I was very upset at my foolishness. Well, better they thought I had committed a sin than knowing the truth, which I was not allowed to tell.

Soon the bell tolled to announce the end of the class. Next we'd be going to the chapel, but first there would be a recess in the courtyard. I hoped no one would ask me anything anymore. I saw Sister Marie-Bernadette take out her rosary beads and start to pray. She walked toward one of the stone benches all the way at the end in a corner. She motioned to me to come over. I knew she would reprimand me for inventing stories.

"Come and sit down near me," she said gently. "I know you were not lying in class before."

I blushed. This was so embarrassing. What was I to do. Insist I lied? Then that would be a lie too? I wished I could ask Yvonne to tell me what to do.

"You don't have to answer me." Sister Marie-Bernadette said, as though she had read my mind. "I could feel you are not the same as the others. You see I too, am different. We're a little lost. Not quite fully at home. Something has been taken from our soul when we had to run and leave our origins. We will always search and wander. Maybe that's God's will? Maybe he singled us out because we are special! We must be grateful to him, and trust his wisdom."

"I don't want to be special, Sister," I said. "I want to be just like the others!"

"You are so young. I can understand it is confusing. Child, if you ever want to speak to me and tell me the story, you can. I will keep your secret. You need not be concerned."

"Thank you Sister. It's chapel time now. God will tell me what to do." I would have loved to tell her the story about Spain. I was glad she knew I hadn't lied, but I wasn't sure she should know for certain. Well, this time I'd really lied. I wasn't going to ask God. Yvonne was my God. I was going to ask her, and I'd do whatever she told me, even if it wasn't what I really wanted.

The bell tolled again. We all marched toward the chapel, heads bent, in single file under the tall arches bordering the courtyard. The statue of Saint Francis in the middle always looked at us. And then, I made my decision. After Mass, I would go to Saint Francis and I'd tell him everything. He was made of stone, but he would hear every word and would never tell anyone. Of this I was sure.

I would tell him what happened after Papa found us and why our heads and feet all had to go together! Over the mountains into Spain. I would tell him the whole story, just like it happened after Papa found us.

Let's see. It was so long ago. Would I remember everything?

"Saint Francis, I know you'll want to know what happened. You watch us go around you all the time, but no one speaks to you. Well now you'll know something very important, something no one else is supposed to know, something very secret. I am so glad you're here, Saint Francis. I really need to tell you what happened."

As I entered the chapel, hands piously clasped together, and eyes lowered, my lips moved with silent words. It looked like I was praying, but in truth, I was already talking to him.

The little village of Cardesse at the foot of the Pyrénées mountains, right on the Spanish border, was peaceful on the outside, but you could feel the movement of the refugees arriving and going, like a stream that flows endlessly.

Today they were here — tomorrow, no more. What happened to them? Where did they come from? Where did they go? It seems no one knew, and no one cared to discuss it.

Papa, now that he was back, made life seem much more normal. I did not care where we were — just that we were together. It seemed so comforting after the endless times of wandering.

Papa had an argument with Maman because she had sold the car. Papa had a passion for cars. He did not care if there was no gasoline, no place to drive, nowhere to go, no food to eat. His beautiful machine was gone, and his heart was broken.

Papa, how much I would have loved to give you back your beloved machine, I thought. "I will someday, I will. I'll find the biggest, shiniest, fastest, machine in the world! Then I'll get a big pink ribbon and wrap your wonderful machine all around! Tie a big bow, with a thousand kisses, and you will ride into the sunset, smiling, happy. You'll see someday, Papa. Don't be sad now. This machine was no longer pretty enough for you anyway!"

Days passed. People came and went in the big house. Then, they disappeared and new ones arrived. One night, late in the evening, two dark men came. They wore black shoes, dark blue sweaters and berets on their heads. They were small but looked strong. They made Papa close the curtain and the light — just a candle on the table. They looked like a secret, a big dark secret.

They whispered around the table and looked strangely at us, as we were huddled in the corner of the room. Much discussion went on about money — per head, per feet, per person, per child, per adult. I listened, fascinated. Was Papa going to sell us? Per head? Per person? Per child? Per adult? Per feet?

Were we worth a whole lot of money?

Was a head worth more than a whole person?

Was an adult worth more than a child?

Was a foot worth anything?

Oh! it was so interesting. I knew Papa and Maman would take good care of us, and I waited for the outcome of the lengthy negotiations.

Then, one of the men started shaking his head and saying that was out of the question. No-no! He pounded the table very hard, with each no.

Papa started asking the man, in a voice that sounded like pleading. He almost had tears in his eyes. "Please, please, try to understand!" he said. "I cannot do it. Please do not ask me that. I cannot."

Papa sounded desperate. I suddenly did not like these men. Why were they making Papa suffer? Why did they want him to do something he couldn't do? Maybe Papa didn't want to sell us? They kept talking about feet that were no good, feet that couldn't walk, feet they didn't want.

They said some legs were small. They would take the small legs and carry them, if necessary. They said some legs were old. They would not take the old legs, because old legs could not run fast enough. But they would take the heads — all the heads, and Papa had to pay for each head.

Papa wanted to shake the older man's hand. The man kept banging on the table, saying "no, no," and he didn't want to take Papa's hand. How could someone not take Papa's hand when he offered it? Such a good warm loving hand!

Finally, the two men left. They said they would return the next night to hear Papa's decision. They looked at us like meat — meat they were going to buy, but couldn't agree on the price. I was happy to see them go. They were not doing what Papa wanted and he looked very sad. I didn't like the way they treated him.

Maybe they would forget to come back the next day?

Maybe they would be gone forever?

Let them buy feet and heads somewhere else, I thought.

They closed the door and vanished in the dark, mysteriously, as they had come.

Now Papa and Maman started talking excitedly. It seemed they had to decide on something before the men returned. All I could do was pray they never did.

Papa and Maman said we would talk about the problem tomorrow, the problem of the heads and the feet. Even I would be allowed to listen! We all went to sleep in our respective corners of the little room.

The next morning we sat around the table. Now Papa and Maman started to explain who the dark men were. They were called *passeurs*. That meant they came to get you at night and walked with you into the Pyrénées mountains, which were very, very high. They knew the mountains well, so they could lead you in the darkness up and up through all the small passages. In the day, you had to go into a hole to hide. You stayed there until night came again.

The *passeurs* would give you cheese and bread to eat so you would not be hungry. If the border patrol soldiers were there during your walking, you would have to run and hide, even if it were in the night.

If the soldiers saw you, maybe they would shoot you while you ran to hide. If they were nice, maybe they would let you turn back from where you came without shooting you.

You would have to do this many nights and many days. The mountains were very tall and there would be much climbing to do, for hours and hours, without stopping. One *passeur* would be in front with a rope. We would all hold on to the rope tightly and not let go so we all stayed together. The other passeur would be at the other end. This way, no one would get lost.

If we climbed fast enough!
If the border patrol soldiers did not shoot us!
If they did not turn us back!
If we did not break a leg, or something else!
If we walked in complete silence!
If we did everything the *passeurs* told us to do!

We might reach the border that connected France to Spain. There, two other *passeurs* would meet us and take us down the mountains into the other side called Spain. We would have to hide going down the mountain the same way as going up, because they also did not want us to come on the other side.

This was all a deep secret. We could never tell anyone about it. If we got to Spain, the Germans could no longer follow. Free Spain was apparently better than Free France.

So then, why was it so difficult to go there?

If Spain had good people, who were not harassed by the Germans, why wouldn't they let us come freely, with happiness? Why did we have to go in the night over the mountains, hiding in holes during the day? Why did the two dark men called *passeurs* have to buy us? Or sell us? Our heads separate from our feet? Why were some heads good, and some feet bad?

We already left our house in St. Gratien.
We already left Mirka to sleep under Big Tree.
We already were hungry, and cold,
and lonely, and afraid.

Couldn't the good people of Free Spain tell us to come? Tell us they wanted us? Couldn't they send a nice car that Papa could drive freely in the day? Couldn't they take us all, heads and feet together?

It made no sense to me. Nobody else was confused. I must be the only one who didn't understand. That was not unusual. Now

Papa asked: Did we think we could do all this? Did we feel strong enough? Were we not afraid?

We all looked at each other and said:

Yes. We would do whatever Papa and Maman said.

If we had to climb, and hide, and run, and they said we should, then we would.

Then, we talked about the *passeurs*, and the one who pounded his fist on the table and said "no, no," and who wanted heads, but not all the feet. Papa sadly explained that the *passeurs* did not like small feet like mine because they couldn't run fast enough and would get everyone shot if the soldiers came. And then, they didn't like old feet like Oma's, because they also couldn't go fast enough and they would get tired and could not go for hours and hours.

The *passeurs* said they would take the small feet, because they could carry them if they had to, but they could not take the old feet, because they knew they could never reach the final destination. So, that meant Oma could not come with us, if we went with them. Oma would have to stay behind, and maybe we could come and get her later when things were better.

No, no, Papa had said to the *passeurs* at the table.

No, no, I felt in my heart.

Now I started to understand why Papa had to pay for our heads, our feet, the young ones, the old ones. I knew we would never leave without Oma, and Papa said he would speak to the passeurs again tonight.

Oma, we will carry you.
We will never, ever, leave you.
Oma, your old feet carry a tower of strength.
Oma, we love you.
Let others go to Free Spain!
If the mountain doesn't want you,
it won't have us either.

When night came the two dark men returned. Papa closed the curtain, closed the light, lit the candle. They sat around the table. Papa took out a package of bills and put them down near one of the *passeurs*.

He said the money was all there. For all the heads and all the feet. The money was double for the young feet and the old feet. That paid for two extra heads.

Papa's eyes were dark and serious. "Please do this for us! We won't let you down."

The older *passeur* shook his head from side to side. He put his hand on the pack of money and pushed it aside next to Papa.

"I am sorry," the *passeur* said, "and you will be sorry too!"

They got up to leave. Now he stretched out his hand to shake Papa's. "Goodbye and good luck!" he said.

Papa looked around the room sadly, stopping his gaze on each of us. It felt as if he knew something terrible was going to happen to us all, and he wished he could stop it, but could not.

Well, as I had thought before:

If he couldn't take the young feet

And the old feet,

Let him go to buy heads and feet elsewhere!

Mass went by so fast. Everyone was leaving the chapel and I was still kneeling. I realized I hadn't prayed. Would I be forgiven?

I looked up at Saint Francis up on the right. He was our patron saint, so his statue was everywhere in the convent. He stood on a tall pedestal under the beautiful stained glass windows. The light filtered through, shining its glow all around him. His hand was lifted, the two forefingers held up in the air.

I think he smiled at me. Yes, I am sure he did. I even saw him moving his hand, as though he was giving me benediction.

"Thank you, Saint Francis," I whispered.

"I knew you would want to hear my story. I am so glad I can speak to you. I have so many things to tell you. We'll be good friends from now on."

Saint Francis's eyes followed me as I left the chapel. He waited for me in the courtyard. I went near and stroke his hand. Sister Marie-Bernadette passed by and smiled at me. I think she knew I had told him. Maybe she went to him as well? To tell him all her secrets.

5

THE
CHURCH
HAS
GAINED
TWO
SOULS

We give you
our children.
We give you
all we have.

Our past.
Our future.
To safeguard.
To hold.

We betray
our faith.
In our hearts
we hope
to be forgiven

The small room in back of the chapel was rarely used. Some-times a group of girls who were having their first communion would gather there before entering the chapel. They slowly walked out, all dressed in white, with a shimmering veil on their head, holding their catechism in one hand and a white flower in the other.

Then, they lined up in front of the altar, kneeled and received communion for the very first time. The little round wafer that contained Christ was placed on the tongue where it slowly melted while you prayed.

"Careful not to bite it," we had been told, "or you will hurt Christ and blood will come into your mouth."

Sometimes the small room was where older girls taking their first vows gathered. That was a very solemn day.

Today, the room belonged to Sister Marie-Valentine. She was

ninety-six years old. A saint, everyone said, a real saint. She had died two days ago and was resting in the little room behind the chapel. A special Mass was given in her honor daily and everyone went to visit her to say goodbye.

This afternoon was our turn. I really would have preferred not to go. I was frightened. I had never seen someone dead before. I knew it would be impossible to find an excuse and so prepared myself for the visit.

We entered the dark room. Sister Marie-Valentine was dressed in her habit. Her face was very pale and appeared so small, all surrounded by the folds of the white coif. There was a strange odor in the room.

We were to walk past her body, stop and pray, then gently kiss our fingertips and deposit our caress on her black robe. We were to say our goodbye to Sister Marie-Valentine. We were to pray for her soul to be in heaven, where it surely was, right next to God.

We could ask Sister Marie-Valentine to do something for us, if we wanted, if we had a special favor, because she could tell God directly now, being so close to him. But we should not be greedy and ask for too many things, because there were others who wanted some wishes.

I stood straight, looking at her closely, so I would know she heard clearly when I asked her for my favor. I would have liked to hold my hand over my nose, because it smelled so bad, but I wasn't going to do that. It was not permissible.

Hello, Sister Marie-Valentine. I hope you are in heaven where they all say you are, because you were so good and you never sinned. I'll never go to heaven, Sister. I sin all the time. I can't help it.

Sister Marie-Valentine, can you help me? I am desperate. You are up there above us all. The whole world is at your feet. Find my Papa and my Maman, please. You can see them, I am sure. Please find them for me.

Sister, my next request is a terrible sin, but if you are a saint you will forgive me, and I will never ask you for anything else as long as I live. I will be satisfied, and I will never sin again. This second favor, and I know I am supposed to ask only one, but the two are connected, is that I become what I was before. You know! Before — before the conversion.

Sister, I am so grateful that Père Agathange let my sister Yvonne and I enter the convent. Papa and Maman had to get his special permission to do that. They agreed we could be converted. It was safer, Père Agathange had told them. There was no choice. They said it was to save our lives. But now, I miss them so, and I miss being what I was before. Please tell God to understand and forgive me. It's not that I don't love him. It's just that I feel different from the others here, and I miss being what I really am.

I was a Jewish child.
I was good.
I was loved.
For nothing. For everything.
Why am I not good anymore?
Why am I a sinner now?
I thought it was all right
to laugh,
and be naughty sometimes...
I never knew sin before.
Just to be me,
just to be me.

Sister, that day, when Maman brought us to the convent, I was so frightened. I remember it just like today.

Life was good in Grenade-sur-Garonne, the little village where we were hiding from the Germans. I had made some friends. I had rabbits and my little pet chicken Kuku.

Then one day, Maman put some clothes in two little bags, some shoes and socks, some other things we needed.

"We must go now," she had said.

"Why, Maman, why? I don't want to go. My friend Sophie isn't going. I like it here. Please, please let me stay," I had implored.

But Maman had not listened. The train to Toulouse took an hour. When we arrived I saw the convent. It looked so big. Its forbidding stone walls seemed to go on and on endlessly. The huge front wooden door was very frightening. The narrow cobbled street, bordered by the canal, made me feel there was no life between the stone building, the water and beyond. My heart was beating hard.

"Maman, don't ring the bell," I had said, trying to hold back her hand from pulling the heavy chain that was hanging on the side of the monstrous door.

"Let's go, Maman, please, let's go!" I had begged.

But Maman had not listened. She quietly proceeded with her plan. A tall figure, all dressed in black, with an enormous white halo of cloth around her face appeared. There was no hair, no ears, no neck to be seen — just eyes, a nose, a mouth, pale, colorless, without expression.

"Oh yes, Madame," the Sister had said. "Mother Marie-Thérèse is expecting you. Please come in."

The forbidding door had parted further to let us in. The entrance hall was somber. Stone floor, dark walls, very high ceiling with no sky above. Straight ahead was another door.

Mother Superior received us. She smiled and was gentle, but I didn't care. Her eyes were gray, her face was pale, her uniform was black. I wanted to run — run.

Let me go, let me go, I thought, before it's too late!

"Please come into my study" Mother Superior had said to Maman.

Now another door closed behind us. I was shivering.

"Yes, yes, I understand," she whispered to Maman. "We will take care of them. We'll take good care. Do not be concerned. It will be safer here, you know. God has given you divine inspiration to leave them here, in our hands."

Maman had turned over the little bags containing our belongings. She had lifted me off the ground and hugged me tight.

"Sunday," she said. "Sunday, I will visit you. Be a good brave girl. Your big sister is here. She will watch over you.

Sunday, Sunday I will visit you."

Then Maman quickly turned and left. I grabbed my sister Yvonne's hand, tightly, not letting go. The inner center back door opened, silently, as if by command.

Mother Superior led the way — down, down somewhere. I knew it was the end. I knew I would never walk out again and be with Maman.

You see, Sister Marie-Valentine, I didn't understand then, but I do now. Please forgive me for asking. I don't want you to think I am ungrateful. Please, listen Sister, I will tell you everything, just as it happened.

In the convent we studied all the catechism, and I didn't mind. But then, I learned about sin and evil, about being good and bad, and I found out there was a heaven, a purgatory, a hell, and that I would have to chose where I would go — that it was up to me to decide, by my actions. I didn't want to be bad, so I tried very hard not to do evil.

I kept a little book. Every day I counted. I used little crosses. So many good deeds on the right side. All the bad thoughts and actions on the left. Each night I prayed I would have enough crosses on the right to make up for the left.

I am always being watched.
The saints look over my shoulder.
Their pictures
inside my prayer book
are staring.
The statues in the church
have eyes and ears.
They breathe.
They see.
They hear.
I became a sinner

who must ask forgiveness,
in confession,
in prayer,
in pleading for mercy.

Sister, I didn't understand it would be so hard to be good. I just thought I was — before, before the conversion.

I was very proud the day we were told we were ready to be baptized. I knew it was a special day. Papa and Maman were coming to the ceremony. I was so happy to see them.

We wore beautiful long white gowns.
Special little crowns on our heads.
The altar was covered with flowers.
The incense.
The chanting.
The anointing.
The sprinkling of holy water.
The beautiful chapel
All candle-lit, for the occasion.
Rejoice!
Rejoice!
The church has gained two souls.

Sister Marie-Valentine, I knew Papa and Maman were pleased with us. We had learned well. We were being converted now. This was our reward.

They stood in back of the chapel. They watched and smiled. They were proud, I thought.

Sister, I was an angel now. I had been reborn. I was free of sin. Just like a new infant. They would love me better now. So I silently prayed:

Look, Maman, Papa.
I am free of sin!
I am an angel!
A true angel!

I know now how to be good.
Please take me back.
I know now how to be good!
They taught me.
You must believe.
I learned my lesson well.
I know what a sinner is.
I am innocent.
I confessed.
Take me back!
Take me back,
please.

The procession ended. It was over. All over.
We walked to Papa and Maman, in back of the chapel. They were very serious and, then, I saw her tears.

"Maman,"
I said,
"Maman, why are you crying?
Look, I am an angel.
Before, I was just me.
But now, I have no sins.
Now, I can go to heaven.
Maman, why are you sobbing?"
Papa stood sternly by. His face was gray, his lips tightly shut. His expression somber.

"Papa,"
I said,
"look at my beautiful gown!
Look at my crown!
I am an angel now.
I could go to heaven.
Aren't you happy for me?"

Maman reached out to touch me. Her tears had smeared the make-up on her face. She was shaking.

Maybe of joy?

Of happiness?

For the beauty and solemnity of the occasion!

And then, Sister, she cried out: "I sold you! I sold you!" And she ran out of the church. And she ran from us. We didn't belong to her anymore.

Sister Marie-Valentine, everything happened after that. Everything terrible.

Papa and Maman were taken away.

We lost each other.

And now,

I don't know what they really wanted.

And why was Papa so sad the day of the conversion?

And why did Maman cry?

And why did she say she sold us?

Sister, I know so many people will ask you to speak to God. I am one of the small ones and we usually come last, but could you try for me soon?"

Emilienne, my companion, was holding my hand and started to pull me along.

"Only one wish. How come it took you so long?" she asked.

"Do you think she hears us?" I said.

"Well of course," replied Emilienne. "Don't you know it's a sin to doubt? Of course she hears us. But she won't listen if you are a sinner!"

And I knew then,

there was no hope.

There was a life,

before,
and there was one,
after.
And that new life,
would stay with me,
forever.
They had sold me,
and they weren't coming back.

I remember
how it was.
Then.

And some part
I shall hold.
And
you shall not
stop me.

I've lost all
but,
the memories.

6

TREASURE
IS
LONG,
SHINY
BLACK
HAIR

If you have no mother.
If you have no father.
If you have no home.
If you have no dog.

And you live in an orphanage.
And you wear a black uniform.
And you eat dark bread.
And you drink sad brews
in little metal bowls.

You are mostly sad.
You are mostly lost.
You are mostly cold.

But if you have long hair.
And if it is shiny.
And if it is silky.

Then,
you have a treasure.
A personal pleasure.
Yours, and yours alone.
To caress,
and to own.

And,
if you have a sister.
Whom you love deeply.
Whom you love wildly.
Your anchor.
Your savior.
Your treasure is shared.

It wasn't much.
But it was ours.
We brushed it.
We washed it.
We watched it grow.

Our link to the past.
A small remembrance.
Of happy things forgotten.
Like the smell of a rose.
Slowly fading away.

In the convent no one had long hair. It was hard to maintain. Having lice was a big threat. Short hair was the rule.

My hair was long, black and shiny. My sister Yvonne had asked the nuns to let me keep it. She had taken personal responsibility for its upkeep.

So, here I was, owning this luxurious mane, amidst heads whose backs exposed bare necks and ears. How sad and poor they looked!

The work to keep my hair in line was enormous, but Yvonne did not care. It was well worth the effort.

Every evening, after all chores were done, we, the small ones, were allowed to visit the big girls' quarters if we had someone there we were related to. I couldn't wait for that moment. The best of the day!

Our time was limited, so as soon as I arrived, Yvonne would sit me on a little chair, take out her equipment and go to work.

A brush, lovingly kept and cared for.

A comb, of strange shape, unlike any used in the outside world. It was black. Not rectangular, but square, with long thin teeth very close to one another.

It was a comb for lice removing. You started at the root of the hair near the skull, taking a little bunch of hair at a time. Then, you pulled the hair slowly all the way to the end. On your shoulder was a little white towel. You looked after each pull to see if some lice fell on it. If any came out, you had to report to sister Marie-Joseph, who was in charge of special treatment for contaminated heads.

This, according to the stage of the problem, consisted of wash in a petrol solution. Overnight soaking in some putrid-smelling mixture. Cutting the hair close to the skull, or complete removal.

You see, lice did not live alone. They made little eggs. So, even if you killed them all, you still were left with the eggs who lived on through all the treatments. They also turned into lice later, when you thought it was all over.

Once you had lice you were disgraced. No one came near you, so as not to catch them. It was shameful. It was awful. Something to avoid, no matter what.

You can see how carefully Yvonne brushed and combed through, strand by strand, hours on end. Then, she parted the hair in the center and made two neat equal braids. They were long and thick. She twisted them twice around my head until they were joined with a small barrette to hold in place.

The only time I ever opened the braids was at night when I went to bed. The long hair flowed free, released from its jail. It rejoiced, its waves shimmering like the sea. I would caress it and wrap it around my shoulders. It looked like silk lying on the pillow. Thick and luxurious. Something from the past, far, far away.

One day, a little black spot fell on the white towel during the combing ritual. To be sure its a louse you put it between your thumb nails and squeeze. If you hear a little snapping click and see a spot of blood, you know what it is.

They usually stick to the skin of your head, soaking life from it. Then, they leave their eggs there. Eventually, they descend further to live among the hair, hanging on to the curls. By the time you catch them, they have usually invaded all areas and hopelessly overpopulated their territory.

Yvonne looked aghast. What to do? "Don't tell anyone!" She

ordered sternly.

The next evening she had prepared an array of chemicals and lice killing techniques that were sure to succeed.

She started the process of soaking. The odors were incredibly strong and could not be suppressed. Soon, sister Marie-Joseph appeared and confirmed she knew this day had to come and had been waiting, fully prepared. "Her hair must go!" she commanded.

Yvonne talked and talked, insisting she could, she would, dispose of the lice. Sister Marie-Joseph agreed, while remarking it was useless. "Go ahead and try!" she said.

She gave my sister the necessary ointments and full technical instructions, with the order to report back with a clean head one week later. The treatment was painful and smelly. I submitted without protest. My treasure was at stake.

One week later, Sister Marie-Joseph came to inspect. She was not satisfied.

"The eggs!" she said. "It must go!" she said. "Come to see me tomorrow at four. Be on time!"

Yvonne looked at her with despair. "Please, give me another week — another week," she implored.

"That's impossible. Bring her at four tomorrow," Sister Marie-Joseph firmly replied.

"Sister, can I do it then? Please could I? It will be easier for her if I do. Please let me do it." Yvonne pleaded.

"Fine. If you wish. Come with her. Be there at four."

Sister Marie-Joseph had this special chair, which was a little higher than normal ones. It swivelled, so you could turn the person in it and cut, cut, without moving. In front was a table. A comb, large scissors and a little hand-machine that shaves necks when you squeeze the handles against each other.

"Sit down," she said.

Yvonne was as pale as a sheet. Her lips were drawn tightly. Her eyes wild.

My sister never cried. My sister never cries.

Please don't cry! I thought.

Let them cut my head with the eggs!

You can't cry! Not you.

I went into the chair.

"Well," sister Marie-Joseph said.

"Go ahead! We don't have all day!"

Yvonne picked up the scissors. Took a strand of the black, shiny, silky hair, lovingly stroking it through her fingers.

"Higher. Up there. Up there." Sister Marie-Joseph pointed to the spot above my ear lobe, way up near my cheek.

I looked at my sister.

Don't cry! Oh! please don't cry!

Not you. Not you.

In her left hand she held the strand of hair. In her trembling right, the huge scissor.

I think she closed her eyes, as she clicked and chopped furiously. Powerless to grab me, with the eggs and everything else, and run out on a magic carpet. Somewhere, far, far away, where such things could never happen.

When I opened my eyes,
I looked down.
Here,
there,
and all around
lay my treasure,
on the ground.

PAMIERS:
THE
PARADISE

D*on't*
take
what I love.

It is mine.
You mustn't
tear my heart,
my soul.

My body trembles
in fear of what
you can do.

My world
is fragile.
In one sweep
you can destroy it.

But,
I shan't let you.
I'll fight to the end.

Against you,
the giant,
the mighty.

I will slide
through your fingers
like air you can't see.
And you shall not know
how I escaped.

Life in the convent in Toulouse was grim. I do not remember one single moment that made me feel I wanted the next day to arrive.

Well, perhaps there was an exception. It was Pamiers. Everyone talked about it. Even though I had never experienced it myself, I had heard many tales and it sounded exciting and wonderful.

Pamiers was a small sister convent in the south, located among farmland. It was surrounded by fields and trees and earth. Every summer, the children from the convent in Toulouse were taken to Pamiers in great big trucks. In Pamiers you could farm, you could feed chickens and other animals. You could smell grass and hug the ground. It sounded like a dream, and we counted the days for summer to come quickly so we could leave for this paradise.

Preparations were made. The excitement was mounting.

As the departure date approached, I suddenly realized things were not as wonderful as I had thought; in fact, they were becoming rather devastating. It turned out that only the smaller children were to go to Pamiers. The older ones remained behind to mind the mother house in Toulouse.

Yvonne would not be permitted to leave. I knew I was cornered. The higher authorities had decided how and where my life would be spent. There was no possibility of arguing, requesting, imploring. The answer would be all too clear.

The small children go to Pamiers.
The older ones stay in Toulouse.
How can a small one like me control her own destiny?
Is there escape in this dark world I live in?
Could I choose to be a rat and creep out through a hole somewhere?
Plotting and crying alternated through sleepless nights and tormented days. I thought:

No one must know how I feel.
No one must suspect.
No one must dream of my plan.
Not even Yvonne.

The day arrived. Freshly laundered uniforms on our bodies.
Brightly shined little black-laced shoes.

How neat we looked!
How same we looked!
How excited we were!
Hundreds with joy.
One with despair.

Each of us held on to our little bag, containing two summer
changes. One to wear. One to wash. A little pair of sandals, for
the walking on earth, for berry picking, for chicken feeding, for
planting and harvesting.

The excitement of expectation and departure was exhilarat-
ing. It was even more so for me. I had a plan! My plan would
either succeed and achieve what I wanted, or, it would fail, and
it would be the end, the bitter end.

Goodbyes were exchanged, doors parted, sweaty palms carrying their load. The large front door was opened, revealing huge
trucks parked alongside the canal, on the cobbled street. My eyes
searched anxiously, locating the truck of my choice.

Yes. That one will do, I thought, picking the last one on the
line.

It looked forbidding, with its army-like cloth pulled tightly
over the top to shield you from the outside. Long narrow benches
on each side would soon be filled with little girls, happy to go
somewhere, anywhere.

I took my place on line, as far down as I could.
Let them leave first, I thought.
They want to go so badly!

The line was moving slowly. Trucks were filling up. All was in order, as planned. The last truck was now being mounted. I kept as far back as I could and when I took my seat I was near the rear and could still see the sky. Motors started humming and coughing. Movement was starting. Yes, we were on our way.

Going to Pamiers, the paradise.

Place of dreams and happiness.

Place of pigs and flowers.

Inside my head voices were whispering.

"You have a plan.

A soul is immortal!

No one can dominate it."

The wheels were rolling, faster and faster. Going, going quickly to Pamiers. In the distance the convent became smaller and smaller. The sisters waved their last goodbyes from afar.

The truck was going full speed. I ran past the ones sitting ahead of me. Flew quickly, like air, like fire. Jumped over the back of the truck. Jumped, and hit the cobbled street.

My mind was at peace now.

Soul, thank you.

They can't force us to go to Pamiers.

To leave Yvonne.

She's all I have left.

Trucks don't scare me. They took Papa and Maman. But this one had no soldiers, no helmets, no boots, no rifles. It had only wheels, and little girls who wanted to go to Pamiers.

My body hurts, sprawled out on the road. It's bruised. I am bleeding. But I can see the truck is going, disappearing in the distance.

"See, we won!" my soul whispered.

"They didn't take us away.

We are still breathing. We are still feeling."

Anxious hands were now lifting my limp body from the

street. Soft voices were whispering, wondering.
   "Why would she prefer to die than to go to Pamiers?"

And so it came to pass
in the convent of Toulouse.
That two sisters,
the older,
and the younger,
left together,
to spend the summer in Pamiers.
Pamiers, the paradise!

Rules
had been broken.
It was inconceivable!

But,
now it was known
that a soul
had discovered its immortality!

You couldn't imprison such a soul!
Nor,
could you
send it
where
it didn't want to go!

8

FOR
ALL
IS
GONE
THAT
WAS
MY
LIFE

It's been almost two years now.
In my dreams I still see
the somber truck,
its shadow like a cloud
that darkened my life.

The boots
the helmets
the rifles
held in steel arms
pointing to no one,
for the victims had no armor
no shields
no defenses.

Am I the grain of sand
that shall be left behind?
The small speckle of nothing?
The meaningless remainder?

The wheels turned
and took all.
Far away.
Far away.
And I shall not
know where
and I shall search
in vain.

For all is gone
that was
my life.

We'd stood there watching, Yvonne and I, not knowing what to do. First, I'd wanted to run and join them, but Yvonne had grabbed my hand tightly like an iron grip, and Maman's arm, through the window of the truck had waved me away. I knew Maman wouldn't tell me to go. I knew this was something different.

I could see Papa through the glass pane too. He sat next to Maman, and from time to time he would stroke her hair, smiling sadly. I knew Papa's smile. This wasn't a happy one. I could tell Papa smiled just to make Maman feel better.

We'd already lived in the convent for almost a year. This was the first time we'd come home to Grenade, the small farming village where we lived. This is where we were told to settle after Papa's attempt to escape to Spain over the mountains had failed.

Grenade was twenty kilometers from Toulouse, an hour by train. One central square, one main street, one large cathedral, lots of trees and earth-covered winding narrow streets, small one-story stone houses. Shriveled ancient women in black dresses hung out of windows, surrounded by cats.

Our house was at the corner, the water pump right across the street. The front door opened onto a narrow hallway. To the left was a room facing the front. Further up, another, with its window looking out to the side street. At the end, a little enclosed garden guarded by stone walls all around. There was a well in the garden, a black hole deep in the ground. It was not in use, just a relic from the past. Things were modern now.

You got your water from the water pump that serviced the whole street.

At the end of the garden there was a shed. It had an inside second level, like a balcony. You could climb on a ladder to get there. Oh, what a spot to hide! The floor inside the house was earth. The cooking fireplace was in the front room. There we put a large wooden table to cook and eat. In the corner, a bed was placed. This became Maman and Papa's bedroom. Oma, Yvonne and I settled in the back room. One bed for the girls, one for Oma, a little island in the middle to get to the window.

Grenade is peach country, farm country, sun country. The Garonne river curves and winds around the village, luring you with its coolness and grace. There, I learned to swim, held afloat by Papa. There, Maman took me, almost everyday, to play in the sand and listen to her singing. She practiced endlessly, enjoying the silence around us and the echo her voice created.

Papa rode out to the farms on his bicycle. He came home with chickens, eggs, potatoes, flour and other foods. Oma and I waited at the window. Whatever he brought back would become the evening's dinner. Oma would let me sit on a little stool and duplicate her chores — kneading, peeling, cutting.

Oma, I learned so much from you!

It was so sweet to see my little roll grow next to your challah in the stone oven, all red with heat.

Life was sweet in Grenade. Running barefoot. Sharing with Papa and Maman's friends, the other Jewish refugees from the north. They played cards, sang songs, reminisced. And there was Sophie, the daughter of a friend. She was my age. We became inseparable. We had fun.

Then, one day, Maman put some clothes in two little bags, some shoes and socks, some other necessities. "We must go now," she said.

At first, when Maman brought us to the convent she and Papa came every Sunday to visit. Later it was no longer allowed to travel from one place to another without special permission, and they could not come.

The convent had several buildings that served different functions. The center open courtyard was surrounded by a covered archway all around. There the nuns walked, heads bent, praying, meditating in silence. Sometimes they chanted in monotonous repetitive tones. In the middle was a garden, lovingly tended. Little stone benches, here and there, were placed along the paths.

A statue of Saint Francis, our patron, stood there to guide us. This was a serene and orderly world of its own. No outsider could penetrate. It was awesome and peaceful, like no other place I had every seen before. It was not a place to play, only to pray, and you knew here to be quiet, serious and reflective.

The left wing was separated from the others. That part was reserved for the "*pensionnaires*," the special name used for boarding students. They were the ones with parents who could pay for a fine education in strictly religious surroundings. They could go home on some holidays. They could have a locker in which to store special things brought in from the outside by loved ones. Things like a cake, some fruits or other precious items to be consumed, once a day, when the Sister unlocked the guarded storage room.

This section is where we lived. Papa and Maman's special treat, at one time, was some sugar and a few eggs. The Sister gave us one a day to share. Yvonne and I debated. What should we do with it? Then we decided. We'd split the white and the yellow in separate bowls. The yellow could be stirred with a bit of sugar until it became an unctuous cream. The white could be beaten until it became fluffy like snow.

"Which do you want?" Yvonne asked.

"I'd like the white," I replied. "It seems to fly, and can be shaped into little mountains with peaks."

"All right." she had agreed. "You'll get the whites!"

We knew there was another world hidden in the bowels of the convent. Other children, a lot of nuns. We never saw them, except in chapel sometimes. I noticed there was a long descending concrete path, bordered by tall wire mesh fencing, that led to a black door from which the nuns who taught us entered and departed. We were not permitted to take that path. The heavy door at the far end held mysteries that fired my imagination. I often stared, trying to guess what went on at the other side.

Strange rituals?

Dungeons?

Prisoners on chains?

Or was it heaven, with little angels flying on their pink wings?

I would have given anything to find out. Only fear kept me from running over there, trying to sneak in. I suspected the space beyond the door might swallow me, and I would be no more.

Maman was very upset not being able to visit anymore, because of the new regulations imposed by our conquerors. She took a job in Toulouse, taking care of an old crippled woman, just so she could be near and see us on Sunday, for a little while. But then Papa was not happy. He didn't want Maman to work as a nursemaid. He wanted Maman home.

Maman came to see Mother Superior at the convent. She said she couldn't live without seeing her children from time to time. She begged Mother Superior to let us come home to visit on special holidays.

And now that day had come. We were going home.

Oh! Joy of joys.

The pump that goes psst...psst,

when you push up and down, and clear water flows out.

Sophie, my friend. We'll play. I am happy.

Madame Durant lived on our street, a few houses up. The Gestapo came mostly in the middle of the night to arrest the Jews. Papa and Maman were not taking chances with us. They asked Madame Durant if we could sleep there. Her house was a safe sanctuary, pure, Catholic. No one would dare to question — not even the Germans.

For the others, who don't belong,

who are in hiding, who are running,

no place gave protection.

They always feared

This would be the night!

The night of the boots.

The night of the flashlights,

searching right into your eyes.

The night of the rifles,

guiding you out and moving you on.
It was on such a night, followed by a morning,
that we walked out and found an empty house,
things scattered about in an unnatural way.

"Yes, they're gone, they're gone," whispered neighbors, sadly eyeing us.

"Go away, go away. Maybe they'll come back for you. Don't stay here. Don't stay here," they repeated.

The main square was lined with townspeople. In the center, a large truck stood. It was surrounded by boots, helmets, rifles. And inside the truck, sat Papa, Maman, many of their friends. Waiting, waiting to go.

Papa, Maman,
I'm running to you,
I'm running to you!
From afar they gestured.
Stay away.
Stay away.

And then, I saw Sophie. She was in the truck, sitting between her parents. Sophie, Sophie, I thought, you've always been the lucky one! They did not send you away, and now you're safe, leaving with them! Sophie, Sophie, how I wished to be you!

Hours passed. We stood, feeling numb, witness to a scene we did not comprehend. And now the truck was moving. Some hands waved from inside. Bye, bye, bye... I looked up to the sky for an answer. Why? Why? Where? Where?

The train to Toulouse takes an hour. The nuns were expecting us. They had been notified. Mother Superior sympathized.

"Yes we are sorry they were taken. We heard. Of course you may stay here! But, you understand, we must move you. Your parents are not longer here to keep you in our *"pensionnaires"* section. We will transfer you to the orphanage quarters. The good charity of the convent will provide for you, as for the other unfortunates who have no one to care for them."

We packed our two little bags.
I looked around and thought:
Goodbye freedom!
Goodbye egg white! Egg yellow!
Goodbye Grenade!
Color.
Papa, Maman, Oma.
Water pump that goes psst...psst.
Goodbye Sophie,
you're free!

"Come on. Let us go." Sister Marie-Madeleine said. Yvonne took my hand, holding it tight. We were led toward the long descending concrete path, bordered by the tall, wire mesh fencing.

It was high,
forbidding,
inescapable.
I shivered.
I trembled.

Now I knew.
Now I knew what was beyond the door.

I wanted to run.
Little by little.
Step by step.
The claws had encircled their prey.
Tighter,
tighter.
And now, they had full possession,
and there was no return.

Terror filled my body
like dark ink running through veins.
The black door beyond
was slowly opening for us.
For the first time.
For the last.

9

TODAY
THE
CHURCH
BELLS
RING
FOR
FREEDOM

Today the church bells ring at odd times. Not for Mass, but for freedom.

Even inside the confining walls of the convent, it is hard to escape the excitement of victory.

Today Mass will be like Sunday. Full of pomp and circumstance. To thank the Lord, thank the Lord who made us free.

What does freedom mean? I wonder. Different things. Strange sensations. Questions. Evaluations. Reflections. What changes will freedom bring? New risks. Discoveries. Am I ready? Can I cope with upcoming surprises?

Will freedom be good? Will freedom be safe? Will freedom be strange? A sensation I've truly never understood. Never had within my grasp. I am scared. Yes, afraid.

The Germans were defeated. They left. Were chased out. Finished. The Americans are here now. Our heroes. To be worshipped. A German can never be defeated. In my mind his image will never fade.

Not him, but his boots.
Not him, but his helmet.
Not him, but his rifle.
Not him, but the truck.
The truck, that took what was dearest to me.
The truck, that took what was safest to me.

No. For me, his victory will remain. He has taken all I had. He won.

In the convent others didn't feel that way. There was much jubilation. A Sunday meal was planned in midweek. We would be permitted to sing. Special songs to rejoice. Special songs of praise.

The chapel would have services continually. You could express your joy without interruption. Celebration was in the air.

Yvonne had come to love the life of the convent. She had expressed her desire to become a nun. I was afraid to lose her to the faith.

I had observed many of the young girls who were very pious. They studied hard and then, one day, they wore a long white gown and a thick cotton scarf around their head to hold the hair in place. As time went on they became more and more serious. They no longer talked and laughed. Just a lot of praying, studying, meditating.

Then, one day, there was a big church ceremony in which they married God, and got to wear a gold ring around the finger of the left hand, like Maman had.

At the end of the service they lay down flat on their stomach in the center aisle of the church, their arms outstretched like a cross. After the numerous blessings from the priest they left, heads bent, fingers gripping rosary beads, chanting in monotonous tones.

When they returned, a little while later, they were dressed in black. Their hair was gone, fully hidden under their white coifs. They no longer looked the same. They were married to God now.

They still had a year to revert back if they couldn't accept the rigorous life they had to follow. Many changed their mind and left the ranks. I do not think life was ever the same for them after that. They had aspired and failed. They were not good enough to be God's wife. You could always be God's child. That was easy — but surely not the same.

I didn't want to lose my sister. It frightened me, but I was powerless. The magnetism of the church had possessed her. Maybe she needed a safe place to belong. But then, she would be gone — a black habit, and a pale face. I prayed it would not happen.

Then, one day, we were summoned to Mother Superior's office. We walked in and stood respectfully at attention, waiting to be addressed. The tension inside made me shrink.

"I have some news for you," said Mother Superior. "Your grandmother is alive. She is not able to travel here but she has requested, now that the war is over, that you leave the convent. She is arranging for you to be transferred to one of the Jewish orphanages that are being set up for homeless children whose parents have perished. You are converted and belong to our faith. It is my duty to inform you of your grandmother's wish. It is up to you to chose what course to follow."

Oma, dear Oma.

We'd hoped she might still be alive, left alone there in the village. We didn't know for sure what had happened after that day, when Papa and Maman had been arrested. All communications had been impossible. I dreamily looked up with joy, knowing I'd see her once more.

Oma.

Oma kneading bread. Oma cooking soup.

Oma darning. Oma knitting.

Oma cleaning. Oma sewing.

Oma being there.

Miraculously, she had survived in Grenade, hiding, waiting, hoping.

When the gestapo had come to the house to arrest us, that cursed night in July, she had come out from the back room, bewildered by the commotion.

"Where are you taking them?" she had screamed.

The Nazi holding the menacing rifle pointed it in her direction.

"Shut your mouth, old woman, or we'll take you along for the ride too!" he had shouted.

It is a mystery why he had not done so. Oma, with her halo of snow white hair, her proud chiseled face with piercing black eyes, might have conjured some memory of an Oma he once had. Perhaps he didn't have the courage to drag her to her death. In that strange moment that determines our fate, hers was to survive, and suffer through.

And now we knew she had survived, and wanted us to leave

the convent. Yvonne had a clear path. She felt she belonged here. What was there to consider? For me, it was different.

I had never belonged. I knew it.

Deep inside. Everywhere.

In all my being.

For me, the fire was burning all the time. I had no peace. I did not know what it was I was seeking, but I knew I wanted to feel, and smell, and be, in so many ways that could never be reached here.

No. I did not belong.

Mother Superior carefully explained we would always be part of the church. We did not have to leave the faith, even if we left the convent. We could test ourselves. We could return any time. It was a road we had to consider carefully. A frightening decision to make, or not to make. It was up to us.

Yvonne waited for me at the end of Mass outside the chapel. "Do you want us to talk?" she asked. I looked up, happy she had asked me. "Yes," I said gratefully. "Wait for me near your dormitory one half hour before changing time. I'll meet you there."

I went early. I felt very strange. Like on the eve of a great adventure when you don't know what will happen, and you feel butterflies in your stomach, in nervous anticipation.

I sat on the edge near the pillow side. My mind was on the box, so close under the pillow. Just last night I had opened it. I had talked to Papa and Maman, telling them about the liberation, wondering where they were.

In the box, I also kept Maman's amber necklace. The one the baker had sent. I still had the little note he had written. I kept it around the necklace, carefully rewrapping it when I put it back. I never would dare to wear the necklace. I just looked at it and caressed it. Just to think she got off the truck to send it made me shiver. She'd sent her gold watch to Yvonne.

"Where are you Maman? These treasures cannot take your place. Where are you?"

In the box I also had the little paper on which Papa had scribbled the note he threw out of the truck when they were leaving Drancy, the concentration camp near Paris, where they took all the Jews and other prisoners from all over France. We never heard after that. These were the last things I had left.

Yvonne entered quietly and sat on the bed, waiting for me to start talking. I waited for her. Finally, she broke the silence and asked me.

"Well, what do you want to do? I don't know where they want to send us now. I don't know how it will be there. I want to stay here."

I looked up, trying not to start crying. I didn't want to make Yvonne do something she didn't want, but I didn't want to stay here either. I didn't want her to become a nun.

"I am not happy here," I said. "It's different for you. You're always good. You do everything you're supposed to, and you're so pious. The nuns love you. I am a sinner. I never do anything right. I always feel I'm bad. I know it doesn't show outside, but I feel that way. I try so hard to be as God wants me, but I can't. Sometimes I have doubts. Sometimes I think he didn't mean for me to feel that way. I think he wants me to really be happy, and not hurt all the time because I am not perfect. Can you imagine?" I exclaimed. "I have doubts! That's a mortal sin. I always think hell is waiting for me. I won't even get into purgatory! Maybe it won't be that way somewhere else. I don't know. I am scared. I'll do whatever you say," I reassured her. "I never want to leave you."

"So you prefer to leave the convent and try living elsewhere?" she asked.

I didn't answer. I took out the box, slowly opened it, lovingly touching its contents.

"I can't even feel free to love what's left. Maybe it'll be different out there, but I'll stay if you want. You know I'll never leave you!"

"I'll tell Mother Superior tomorrow that we'll go. I'll get you settled. Then we'll see," she said.

I looked at her, with all my love, stored so deep inside. She didn't like me to be too demonstrative, so I didn't jump and kiss and hug her, as I would have loved to do. Such behavior was not looked well upon in the convent.

"I am afraid of leaving, but I think we should try," I said, happy she had agreed.

I knew Yvonne would have little doubts if it were not for me, but she felt responsible for my life. She could always resume her new calling after she found me a place.

A place where I could exist.
A place where I could breathe.
And so, we decided to try.
Try, to touch a new world outside.
A new world of mysteries.
A new world of readjustments.
Of frightening discoveries.

The date of our departure was set. We were not really leaving. Many strings were tied with invisible knots. They held us to the anchor. The anchor that had sheltered and saved us. We were not thrown to the wolves.

And there was a return, if we wanted.

I've seen darkness
But now, no more.
Smile.
Be happy.
Freedom has come.

But, how can I?
And,
why should I?
Having lost all.

10

IT
WAS
JUST
YESTERDAY,
THIS
NEW
LIFE
STARTED

The Jewish orphan's home that claimed us was sending someone to pick us up. It was a rainy midweek morning.

We had packed two little bags. We were dressed in our Sunday best. We sat and waited, knees folded neatly under our mid-calf skirts.

Mother Superior sat behind her desk. Her *pince-nez* tightly squeezing the bridge of her nose. She busied herself with papers, but I could see she was disturbed — not her usual composed self.

I suddenly remembered that day, some years ago, when Maman had first brought us here. How frightened I had been. How horrified to be left in her care. She had seemed so cold, so distant.

I had gotten to know her better. Not that you could address her lightly, or laugh in her presence, but now I understood her burdens. How she always had to make the ultimate decision. How hard she tried to be firm, but fair. How difficult the choices were, sometimes.

A Sister could forget, could joke and be funny if it was a good spring day and the sun shone. But Mother Superior never could, and when she entered a classroom, the dining room or the chapel, a hush floated in the air, all breaths held in silence.

She was most interested in us. The new souls God had gathered in his eternal search. These souls were in her care. She had guarded and nurtured them, and now danger was threatening her charges.

She lifted her head every few minutes, looking up at the large black and white clock on the wall, pen held in hand. She absent-mindedly dipped it into the ink well too frequently, and a big blotch fell on the papers in front. She carefully cleaned it, rocking the blotter back and forth many more times than needed.

Mother, I feel that way too. I would have liked to tell her, knees shaking slightly against the wooden chair. I said nothing.

He walked in without hesitation. He was a young man, in his twenties. His hair was curly and unruly. He was wearing a hand-knit sweater with a rolled collar, simple corduroy slacks, sporty shoes, a short loose jacket that could double as a raincoat. He had a kind face. He smiled.

He seemed quite at ease as he greeted Mother Superior. Not intimidated. Very calm. How could that be? I thought. Doesn't he know Mother Superior is the ultimate being here, before God? That you feel a slight shiver in her awesome presence?

No. He did not seem to see this. He casually discussed some details concerning our move, and thanked her for having kept us until he came to take us back.

It seemed he felt it was his destiny, today, to reappear in our life, to claim us. As though we belonged to him.

We stood there, watching. Neat, in our little black uniforms, stockings and black laced shoes, navy cape and small berets. What did we have in common with him anyway? He, with his unruly curly hair? His assured airs?

Suddenly, I felt it was all a mistake. We were leaving our safe haven for chaos. I would have liked him to go away. Leave me be to turn back. To open the door and re-enter the inner enclave. But I was frozen in the moment. And could not express my will.

We each picked up our little bag, silently saying goodbye to Mother Superior, feeling pangs inside.

Mother, we'll come to Mass on Sunday.
Every Sunday.
Mother, we'll say our prayers
every day without fail.
Mother, we shall not sin.
Mother, we will not abandon our faith, and you,
who are all we have now.
Mother, we'll be back.
Mother, we'll return."

He looked amused. A slight smile seemed to dance in the corner of his eyes. He said nothing.

Mother Superior embraced us. It was the first time. I felt her heart beating under the black habit. Her eyes were sad. I could almost feel tears would fill them if she would allow it. She blessed us, said a prayer. We all crossed ourselves. Sisters Marie-Bernadette, Marie-Catherine and Marie-Lucienne were standing outside her office, waiting to say goodbye. We belonged to each other now. Yvonne and I had traveled the hard roads of discovery, guided by their spirit. Learned the faith, the sacrifices, the power of redemption. And now, we were being reclaimed, snatched away. Would the new road be as difficult to follow?

Mother Superior had a present for us. A new set of beautiful rosary beads, pearl white and shiny, not like the plain brown ones with which we normally said our prayers, one after the other, as we slowly advanced on the long endless string.

A new prayer book was also given, with a soft black leather cover. The red silk string to hold the page shining bright. The gold leaf on three sides gleaming, still fresh and untouched. I had always wanted one like that. Only the Sisters had them. A special gift on the day of their vows, to be treasured forever. The razor-thin pages were transparent like parchment. The beautiful black printing like velvet trimming to feast your eyes on. I always thought it would be easier to pray in such a book. And now, I had one of my own.

Mother Superior, I'll be eternally grateful to you for this precious gift, I thought. I solemnly took the gifts and thanked her, eyes downcast, not wanting to show my pleasure. Being too joyous for a material possession was sinful, even for the book of God.

And then she handed us the letters. "They're yours to keep," she said with tears in her eyes. "Your parents' sacrifice was enormous. I wish they'd been able to come back for you." Carefully opening the yellowed pages with trembling hands we read:

We: Fersztenfeld Maurice and Fersztenfeld Hana, undersigned, declare we entrust our two children:

1) Yvonne and Renée to Father Agathange Bacquet, Chaplain of the

Franciscan monastery of Port Saint-Sauveur in Toulouse so that they may continue their education in that establishment.

We authorize our two children to be instructed in the Christian religion, and to receive baptism if they express the desire of their own free will.

We, furthermore, pledge that we will do nothing to make them deviate from observance of said religion in the future.

Having full confidence that our two beloved children will be surrounded by kind solicitude from both the Father Chaplain and the Franciscan nuns, we fully discharge them of any responsibility for any accidents that may occur.

Toulouse, October 3rd. 1942

M. Fersztenfeld
A. Fersztenfeld

(Original letter in Photo/Document section)

Remit urgently
To the Convent of the Franciscan Sisters
Port-St. Sauveur, Toulouse

To Sister Marie-Beatrix

July 11, 1943

Our kind and dearest Sister,

Alas! What we expected has happened. The German police is holding us, my poor wife and I. Have pity of our poor children, our beloved Yvonne and Renée. Keep them and protect them, because they are alone. We hope that God will one day let us see our darling little girls.

We are for the moment in the military prison behind the Théâtre Royal right near you, but it is possible that from here we will be transported to Drancy.

Please inform my poor mother. We have courage and are bearing our unhappiness with dignity. Our kindest thoughts for Mademoiselle Huron and most particularly for our good Mother Superior and to Father Agathange.

May God keep you and save us. We have nothing with us. No underwear, no clothes, nor money. Everything was taken from us. We thank you with our whole heart. Oh! how great is our misfortune, but we do not lose hope. A better day will come.

Adieu, our Dear Sister.
Pray for us.

(Original letter in Photo/Document section)

A last look.
A last goodbye.
A pinching of the lips.
A tightening of the jaws.
The large front door opened for us.
We were outside.

The young man took my hand to cross the street. I felt a strange sensation, as though my stomach was falling down. Only Papa ever held my hand before — no other man since. That was so long ago. I hardly remembered.

How I wished now this hand was Sister Marie-Marceline's, that I had held so many times as we ran to the fields that blissful summer in Pamiers. She was full of gaiety and loved to sing as we marched through the country dirt roads, holding our little straw baskets, waiting to be berry-filled.

She frequently took two little ones by the hand as she led the caravan up front. I always ran to be there when her extended hands searched for the small fingers to hold on to.

That summer in Pamiers, for which I had almost lost my life jumping off the truck, because Yvonne was not permitted to come along, had turned out to be the only carefree time I remembered in the convent. I had almost forgotten how lonesome I was, surrounded by nature and its smaller creatures.

This hand was different. It was large and firm like a big glove. More like a mitten, in which your fingers were imprisoned. His voice was husky, like the Father's who came to say Mass. It had a strange echo of things I remembered in a cloudy way.

He walked straight and addressed us. He said his name was Jean. He said we should call him that. Not Mister. Or Sir. Or Brother Jean. Just Jean.

He made long steps as he walked. I had trouble keeping up. Nothing seemed to phase him. He — with the curly unruly hair, who looked so out of place dragging along two navy blue capes and tidy black stockings. Our world was not his. His world was not ours. What were we doing here sharing this street?

We took a bus to the other end of town. Yvonne looked concerned. Hopefully we would not go too far from the convent. As far as she knew, she would soon resume her training and her avowed vocation. Just to see me settled first; that was her main concern.

"Your names? What do they call you?" Jean asked.

"Yvonne," my sister said under her breath.

"Renée," I whispered hesitantly.

Was he actually going to call us by our first names?

Was he actually going to talk to us?

We didn't even know each other!

Who was he anyway? Where was he taking us? Suddenly, fear set in. We shouldn't have left. What a fool I was. If not for me we'd still be there. Safe. My sister knew the answer all along. I should have listened. I wished I had, now.

In the bus.
In the street.
With someone unknown.
Going nowhere.
Without a nun to hold on to.

Without the convent to return to.
Without the church.
Without the strength.

It was just yesterday,
this new life started.
And now again,
you take it all.

I long
to cling
to what I know.
So let me be.

11

LE
CHATEAU

Now once again
all is changing.
The road looks curved.
I see no end.
No sky.
No earth.
As I look
all around
wondering.

The days had melted
one into the other.
The weeks
the months
the years
passed.

Memory faded.
I was this new being
now.
With rules
and paths
to follow.

It was clear.
All was gone
of what I'd been
before.
I had started
to forget
so I could
live in peace.

Silently, I looked around as the bus traveled through town. Finally, we got off and started walking some more.

Then, we were facing a very large house. It looked like a castle. No gates. No enclosing walls. No monstrous front door. Just a big beautiful house.

"Here we are!" Jean said cheerfully. No bell to ring. No lock to undo. No one to open the door. He just walked in. We walked behind him.

"Come, I'll take you to Gisèle" he said.

We looked, puzzled.

"Madame Gisèle. She is the *Directrice* of Le Château. That's the name of our home," he added, seeing our confusion.

"You mean, your Mother Superior?" we asked.

He laughed out loud.

"Yes. I guess that's it. She is our mother. Yes, mother of us all!"

The big center hallway, as you entered, was full of children of all sizes and shapes. Girls, boys. I couldn't believe this confusion. Their clothes were all different. Multi-colored. Their hair was long or short, curly or straight, each one unique. No braids. No tight little chignons. No short cropped cap, cut just below the ear. No stockings. Just bare legs and little socks, dancing in shoes of various colors and styles.

It looked very confusing. They stared at us while they rushed wildly by. We were the funny looking ones for them!

A tall girl passed and rushed up to Jean, encircling him in her arms. Her red curls flowing free down her shoulders.

"Jean!" she exclaimed "I've been looking for you all over! Where have you been? Come with me. I need you in the recreation room. We are setting up for the party. We need more tables and chairs. Come and help!"

"Gabrielle," he said, "I can't right now. I have to find Gisèle. I went to pick up newcomers. Let me introduce them. This is Yvonne, and her sister Renée."

He pushed us forward to shake her hand. We stretched out

our right arm, and curtsied slightly as she shook our finger tips, reluctantly presented.

"*Bonjour Mademoiselle*," we whispered.

"God, where did you get them from?" she said, as she eyed us with surprise.

"Gabrielle, I'll see you later," he whispered.

For the first time I felt some embarrassment in him. Some sadness.

"They are ours, Gabrielle. They are ours — can you believe it?" he added, as though some shame was attached. As though we were to be pitied.

This girl, Gabrielle, was carefree, beautiful. She reminded me of things. Things stored in memory. Like the color of her hair, and a certain scent, of fresh flowers, of green pines.

Something of the past had returned.

Something of sun shining through curls.

Something of a scent, enchanting your senses.

Something of pleasure not being sin. Shameful. To be forgiven. To fight against.

We followed Jean down the hall. The white door had a sign haphazardly painted with the word: **DIRECTRICE**.

It was wide open. You didn't have to knock.

The huge desk in the corner was covered with books and papers. Some small children were sitting on one end of the rug drawing pictures with color crayons. The large bay windows were open onto a wild-looking garden, full of unkept trees and flowers.

Her big bush of white hair was loosely tied with chignon pins. Her large black eyes and thick eyebrows looked kindly toward us. Her fleshy lips parted in a smile full of happiness. Her stocky body, in plain blouse and skirt, moved swiftly as she ran when she saw us enter.

She embraced us. "Welcome, my children. Welcome!" she exclaimed.

"Bonjour, Madame."

"Just call me Gisèle. I wish you happiness in your new home! Do as you please. Feel free. We are here to help you. Come to see me anytime. Just walk in."

"Thank you, Madame Gisèle. Thank you."

And I thought:

May we go now? May we take the bus? Back to safety.
Where Mother Superior has a door you have to knock on.
Where your Mother is not: "Just call me Gisèle!"
Where rules are clear.
Where a uniform makes you feel safe.
Where you are like all the others.
Where the bell tells you it's time.
Where the church beckons you to seek answers,
when you need them.
Reaching inside your soul.
Looking for solace and forgiveness.
While kneeling, head bent,
resting against your finger tips.
Your outstretched hands, palm to palm,
pointed to your forehead.

Jean took us upstairs to the second floor, where the bedrooms were. He saw some older girls in the hallway and called them over.

"This is Yvonne," he said. "Please take her where there is room. She will be living with us. Make sure she has what she needs."

Then he took my hand and walked to the other side of the corridor. He looked into several rooms. He seemed hesitant. At one point he smiled and said: "Ah yes, that will do!"

We walked in. Four girls were sitting around and looked up as we entered. "This is Renée. She is going to live with us," he said. He sat on one of the beds and waited for the introductions.

"Hello. My name is Sarah, and this is Nicole and Rachel and

Simone. This can be your bed — there, near the window. If you don't like it we can change, and you can choose another one."

Jean stood up and said goodbye. He said we would see each other later, in the dining room. I looked at him with apprehension. Was he leaving me here? With them? I guess he was. I walked over to the bed they had assigned to me and put my little bag on it. I waited.

Sarah seemed to be the liveliest of the group. She started talking fast, volunteering information I was not seeking, and asking me questions:

"Tell us. What happened to you? Were you abandoned? Did you lose everyone? Were you left all alone? Have they all perished?"

I did not answer.

She continued. "I came here three months ago. I was in this farm in Dordogne. My parents left me there. I was five years old. My younger brother was a baby, and they had to keep him with them. My parents never returned. I never saw them again. Their names were found in some documents that say they all died in a concentration camp.

"They say my mother and my brother were killed as soon as they got to the camp, because he was a baby, and they did not let mothers with babies live. They killed them with gas. Then they burned them in an oven. My father died too. They don't exactly know where. My new parents in the farm wanted to keep me, but the Jewish agency insisted and they came to pick me up and bring me here. Soon, I'll go to Palestine, if we can get smuggled in."

"Shht, Shht," the other girls whispered. "You know we are not supposed to say... You know you must not talk about it!"

"Oh, she won't repeat it. Jean said she is one of us. Anyway, why would she be here otherwise?"

Then she faced me and said: "And now, tell us. What happened to you? Were you abandoned? Did you lose everyone? Were you left all alone? Have they all perished?"

I did not reply.

Simone came forward and started talking. She was wearing thick lenses fitted into round-rimmed glasses.

"Not me, I was not on a farm. One day my father and mother went to the store to get some food. Then, I didn't see them anymore. They did not come home. The next day, I went looking in all the shops. The woman who owned the sewing store took me in the back.

"She told me my parents had been arrested by the Germans and I should come to live with her family. She showed me this closet and said I would have to sleep there during the day, so no one would know I was there. At night, I could come out and stay in the back room of the store, but without light, so as not to attract attention. I didn't know what else to do, so I stayed with them.

"I never saw the light for all this time. So when they said it was all right to come out, because now we were free, I couldn't see anymore. Now I must wear these special glasses. They told me my parents died in the camp. This is my home now."

"And now, tell us. What happened to you? Were you abandoned? Did you lose everyone? Were you left all alone? Have they all perished?"

I did not reply.

Rachel was getting ready to tell her tale, but suddenly they noticed the time and in unison shouted: "Let's go to dinner. It's time!"

I had not said a word. I was wondering how they knew about dinner? I had not heard a bell, or any other call.

"Come on. Put something else on. You look like a ghost in this black frock," Nicole said.

I think she regretted saying it, because she looked at my little bag and realized there wasn't much to take out from it that would change my appearance.

"Well, we'll take you to the sewing room tomorrow. You can pick out something nice, in any color you like. We'll go with you. Don't worry!"

They dragged me down the stairs. We entered the dining room. I looked around bewildered.

No long refectory tables with benches on which you sit one next to the other. No island in between the tables, so the bigger girls could pass with the hot cauldrons of food.

In the convent, two girls held the handles on each side, and another one would ladle out the food or drink, going from plate to plate.

This dining room had tables all over, without specific plan. Some were bigger, some were smaller, and each person got an individual chair, not a piece of bench. The plates were earthenware, not metal. Some had tablecloths, some were bare. I just couldn't believe the confusion.

Children of all ages, both girls and boys, were running around from one area to another. They were sitting down here and there without apparent order or command from anyone.

In the corner of the room I saw Madame Gisèle's table. She was surrounded by some other adults and a few children. Yvonne was sitting with young people her own age. I glanced over, but was afraid to go near because I would have to speak to her in front of the others, and I didn't want to.

Sarah sat me down at a table and some of the children looked at me curiously. There was no food anywhere, and I wondered how the servers would get through amidst this chaos.

Then, they opened two large doors at one end of the room, and everyone took plates from the tables and went there. Sarah thrust a plate in my hand and told me to follow her.

The room beyond the open doors was like a huge kitchen, with large tables laden with food. Chunks of bread. Drinks. All was laid out to be taken at will. I could not comprehend it, and just stood there not taking anything.

It reminded me of our table in Grenade, that time when Papa and Maman had opened a restaurant at home. *Chez Fersen!* they called it, and we had laughed so when we started to see the first guests coming.

Yvonne and I were not allowed to eat in the restaurant. Oma
would serve us before the others came, and Maman always
picked out the nicest pieces for us.

When I had asked Maman why people were coming to eat in
our room, she had explained: "You see, we must use the ration
tickets to get any kind of food. Money is not enough. You know
the little stamps I give you for the baker when you pick up the
bread?"

"Yes," I had replied, fascinated by the explanation.

"Well," Maman continued. "No one ever has enough to buy
as much food as they need. So Papa asked all our friends if they
want to put the tickets together in one batch. Then he goes to the
farm — you know Monsieur Petonc where we go for eggs,
potatoes and also get a chicken sometimes?"

"Yes. Yes." I shook my head, not wanting her to stop.

"Well, with all the tickets together, Papa can buy more than
each one could separately. Then he brings the food home. Oma
and I cook, and we can make better dinners than if each family
cooked alone, because they can only get one thing, not a few all
together as we can, with all the ration tickets. You see, it's quite
simple," she said, hugging me tight. "And then, I can have nicer
things to eat for my babies, so you can get tall and strong, like a
big tree." She laughed loud, showing me how big, all the way up
to the ceiling!

I loved going to the farm with Papa. He took me on the seat
of his bicycle, in the back. Oma put a little pillow on it, so it
wouldn't hurt my backside. Sometimes I asked Papa if I could
ride up front, and he would let me sit on the handle bar, holding
me between his two arms while he rode the country dirt roads
from one farm to another.

One of my favorite was Mémé Grange's farm, where we got
fresh milk. Mémé would let me sit on a little stool and pull the
cow's nipples to get the milk out.

"See, it's easy!" she'd say, as she showed me how to squeeze,
and the warm, foamy liquid would come out.

The cows were so big. Black and white with spots that looked like maps. Their huge black eyes were loving. They turned their head sometimes as we pulled the nipples. They seemed pleased we took their milk. They never moved, except to swing their long tails from left to right to chase the flies.

Mémé Grange always gave me a little treat when I came. Her grandson, Jeannot, was bigger than I. Sometimes, he'd come over and talk to me. He'd look at my pretty sandals and white socks, and say how nice they looked. Jeannot always ran around barefoot. I wasn't sure he ever took his clothes off to wash or sleep, because they were always the same, and the suspenders that held up his short pants were all frayed around the edges.

In the early evening, Papa and Maman set up the restaurant in the back room where we slept. They pushed the beds in the corner and put a big table in the middle, with long benches on each side.

The guests came in the front door. Papa greeted them and escorted them to our room. Oma and Maman were very busy in the front room, cooking and preparing to serve. They let me bring in some things too, mostly the ones you couldn't drop and break — like the bread baskets or some fruits, if we had any.

I loved the restaurant. Everyone always said: "How nice the children are!" And they would pat me on the head affectionately when I walked by.

Sometimes I heard Papa talking with one of the guests and he'd say: "You must bring the stamps tomorrow Monsieur Frankel. Please don't forget." And then he said it again the next day, and the next, to several of our guests.

Then, one day, Maman said I didn't have to put all my things away today because we were not setting up the table for the restaurant.

"Why Maman?" I asked.

Maman explained, and I felt so sad.

"The guests are not bringing enough ration tickets. They come to the restaurant at night, but they keep the stamps to buy things themselves for lunch or breakfast. So Papa cannot buy enough to cook for everyone. Oma and I cannot prepare without ingredients. So we must close the restaurant."

That was not a happy day for me. But then, Maman would have more time now and we could go to the Garonne river again, where she could sing, practicing the latest melodies from the illustrated colored sheets with music notes on them.

Everyone had some that they had taken along when they left Paris, and they exchanged them with each other. The song sheets were like a double folder. On the cover was the title in big letters and the picture of the singer who made the song famous. Then, inside, were the words printed below the music notes, which were funny-looking dancing designs. Sometimes I heard the same song on the radio, and I would say to Maman: "You sing it much better, Maman. You should be on the cover!"

The person I missed most at the restaurant was Monsieur Zalis. He had no wife, so he always came alone. He was so glad to have company, because he had no one to talk to at home.

Monsieur Zalis always came a little early, before the others. Everyone was busy setting up, so he'd usually keep company with me.

"Do you already know the numbers?" he'd ask. And then, he'd pull some paper and a big black pencil from his pocket, and he'd draw letters and numbers and made me repeat what they were.

Monsieur Zalis walked in the village, talking to everyone. We always met, at the baker, at the dairy, and on the square where the market came on Saturday. He'd sit on one of the benches and wait for someone to come near, so he could talk to them.

Monsieur Zalis always used to tell me when we met: "Your Papa and Maman are the best. You're lucky to belong to such a fine family. So fortunate!"

It is Monsieur Zalis who sent the Germans to our house to arrest Papa and Maman.

The Nazi was wearing a plain suit like everybody. He saw

Monsieur Zalis on the square, and he said: "I just arrived from the north. I am looking for some Jewish families, to convey the latest news. Can you tell me where they live?"

And Monsieur Zalis had said: "I'll take you to the best family we have here. The very finest. You can talk to them, and they'll give others the information."

And Monsieur Zalis proudly showed our house to him, and the Nazi said thank you. And then he sent the soldiers to arrest Papa and Maman.

Everyone in the village had talked about it afterward. How Monsieur Zalis had sent the Gestapo to arrest the nicest family in the village — the ones who had been kindest to him.

Sarah pushed my arm to get my attention. "What do you want? Chicken? A boiled potato?"

Since I had not yet spoken, she wasn't sure I ever would. She shrugged her shoulders and just kept putting on my plate the same things as was on hers. I followed her.

When we returned to the table I stared at the food. I felt a little sick — and very much lost.

Madame Gisèle was going from table to table visiting "her" children. When she reached ours she exclaimed: "Ah! Here is one of our newcomers! Are you being shown around? Have you made some friends?"

"Yes, Madame Gisèle. Thank you Madame Gisèle," I replied.

Some children at the table started to giggle, and she looked at them reproachfully.

"Well, tomorrow you will come to see me, and we will decide in which classroom you belong."

"Yes, Madame Gisèle. Thank you Madame Gisèle."

"Ah, yes, you will also start in the beginners' class to learn Hebrew. We all must speak Hebrew. It will be our national language. We must be prepared!"

"Yes, Madame Gisèle. Thank you Madame Gisèle."

I started to feel worse and worse.
Tables where you sit at random?
Food to be chosen, and taken at will?
Talk going on everywhere? Loud and confusing.
Madame Gisèle addressing me in front of everyone?
Hebrew? National language? Palestine?
Would it ever end?
This eternal search for belonging?
And what would come next?
I wondered.

I stood up, overcome by it all, not knowing what to make of it. Sarah must have seen I was feeling ill. She accompanied me out, and we went upstairs.

We sat on the bed. She took my hand. And then, she looked deep into my eyes and asked once more:

"And now,
tell me.
You must tell me.
What happened to you?
Were you abandoned?
Did you lose everyone?
Were you left all alone?
Have they all perished?"

12

YOU CAME, AND TOOK MY HAND

Y*ou came,*
and took my hand.
Here.
Out of the cold world
I lived in.
You opened your door.
Your heart.
And let me in.

I tasted
the sweetness
of freedom.
Forgotten.Gone.
So long ago.
I thought,
forever.

It was as though
you
had returned life
to me.
Simply.
Without claims
and complications.
To discover
again,
who
I really was.

I had never shown the contents of the box to anyone. Only Yvonne knew it existed. I looked at Sarah. She could be trusted. "You must tell me!" she had insisted.

I opened the small bag and took out the box. "I'll show you," I whispered. First, I took out the picture. "That's Papa," I pointed. "Isn't he grand? That's Maman. Isn't she beautiful?"

I stroked their heads carefully with my fingers, as I usually did when I took out the picture. "Only we are left," I said, pointing to Oma, Yvonne and myself in the photograph.

"We were a family once. We had a house. We had a dog. Her name was Mirka. She was my best friend. The neighbor killed her with a shotgun when we ran to the South of France. She is sleeping under Big Tree at home, where we buried her. I'll never see her again either."

Sarah looked at me, staring into my eyes. She didn't say a word. She just waited for me to go on. Slowly she reached over to take my hand and gave it a little squeeze. She wanted me to continue. She wanted to know everything.

Then, I took out the necklace, lovingly stroking its shiny amber beads. I kept the necklace in a soft brown tissue paper, which I had saved from the wrapping of a book. I hadn't worn the necklace, never even tried it on. To me, it wasn't jewelry. It was just something precious Maman had sent me. The only thing I had left that belonged to her.

"How did you get it?" Sarah asked.

"Maman wore it when she was arrested," I said. "Sometime later we got a note from a baker in a small village. He said Maman had come into his bakery on the pretense of using the bathroom. She gave him the necklace and her gold watch. She scribbled our names and address on a scrap of paper.

"The gold watch is for my oldest daughter Yvonne. The necklace for my youngest Renée," she said. "I beg you to send them. They are the only things I have left for them. Tell them I love them, and not to forget."

The baker, in the letter he sent us, tried to remember exactly the words she used. He had looked outside. She had pointed to the truck. He saw the Germans and the rifles. He knew these convoys. They passed his bakery on their way up north filled with Jewish prisoners.

"My husband is there too," Maman had said, pointing to Papa sitting near the window. "I can't run. I must return."

In his note to us, the baker said how sad he felt, how beautiful she was, how much he would have loved to help her. He had taken the necklace and the watch. He had promised her. "Yes, yes, I'll send these to your children. I'll tell them what you've said. God be with you."

He watched Maman mount the truck. Papa took her two hands and kissed them, and she whispered something in his ear. He caressed her beautiful blond hair, and they both looked out to the baker. In this short instant, the baker said, he knew all they wished to say. He felt he was possibly the last person on earth that would reunite us for a breath — a faint reminder of what we'd lost, scattered as we now were, like dust.

"My Maman was pretty.

My Maman had blue eyes.

My Maman had blond hair.

She loved dresses with flowers.

She liked to sing.

I miss her.

I want her back," I told Sarah.

Sarah was so quiet, not like before when I first met her. "Go on," she said softly. "Tell me everything."

So I took out the note. Papa's scribbled letter. The one he had thrown out from the window of the truck when they were driven out from Drancy, the concentration camp where all prisoners were taken. It was written in pencil, in Papa's fine beautiful handwriting; each word like a painting, each letter like a song. Attached to the note was a stranger's letter. The kind man who had picked up Papa's note and sent it on to us.

First, I handed Sarah the letter from Monsieur Jacques.

Drancy July 19, 1943

Sir,

I live in Drancy near the concentration camp. While going to the market Sunday, yesterday, I passed several cars taking away some men and women of that camp, when a gentlemen who was in one of those cars signaled to me that he wanted to throw me a card.

As I shook my head to indicate my acceptance he threw a note he was holding in his hand. I therefore picked it up and wanted to copy it but it is probably preferable that I send the note itself to you because you will no doubt recognize the handwriting of this gentleman, and will more easily believe this sad message from a person who no doubt is dear to you.

Sincerely,
B. Jacques

(Original letter in Photo/Document section)

And then I handed Sarah Papa's note, so she could read what it said:

July 18,1943

The person who will find this note is kindly requested to notify Mr. Kessler in Grenade sur Garonne (Hte Garonne) that Mrs. and Mr. Ferstenfeld have been deported to Poland.

In doing this you will render an immense service because we have been separated from our two children without any hope of ever returning.

Thank You!
For your noble gesture.

(Original note in Photo/Document section)

Papa's note was yellow and faded. The small piece of cardboard on which he had written it was more than two years old now. My hand trembled as I slowly folded it to make sure it didn't smudge.

"Did you ever hear after that?" Sarah asked. I shook my head.

"That was the last time," I said, as I returned the treasures to the box, carefully rewrapping each and replacing them in their usual corners.

"And then?" asked Sarah.

"And then..." I said.

The others were coming up to the room. Sarah took my hand when she heard their steps in the hall.

"Here, take this sweater. Let's go outside quickly," she said. She ran out pulling my hand until we reached the garden through the back steps. Sarah threw something on the ground and pulled me down next to her.

"Go on," she said. "Go on. You must."

Hours went by as I spoke, uninterrupted. The sun rose softly above the trees.

"We can go in now," Sarah said. Now, Sarah knew everything.

After that night Le Château really became my home. I could speak to them now. I felt I belonged. I knew what they wanted. For us to be what we'd been before. To send us to Palestine. To build a new nation. To forget the nightmares of the past. Slowly, as time went on, I understood and was grateful.

They gave me a pretty dress.
It wasn't fancy,
but it was blue.
They gave me my bare legs,
little sandals that freed my toes.
They gave me a ribbon,
to let my hair flow free.
They gave me smiles,
laughter.
Your lips part and curl,

your teeth shine and twinkle.
They gave me a warm hand,
a caress.
They gave me hope.

Yvonne made some friends too. She waited. Her world was divided. Choices were to be made. Yvonne wasn't sure. Where did she belong now? To the Church? To the Château?

Life in the orphanage was like passing through a narrow channel. On one end you entered, walked, groping in the dark. You were guided this way and that, reminded of your past, informed of your future, and then, when you reached the end, you knew what destiny awaited. Who you were. Why it had all happened and what your place in history would be. Light shone at the end of the tunnel — or so we thought, having little else to hope for.

Gisèle was very busy in an underground network that tried to send Jewish children into Palestine illegally. In her office were pictures of striking men whose faces haunted you, and to whom she spoke aloud whenever she had a problem.

One had bushy white hair and a round kindly face. Another had a pointy beard. They seemed to smile at us and say: "Come on and join us. We're waiting for you."

The photographs were personally dedicated.

"Dear Gisèle, To our struggle — soon to be over."

"Gisèle, Thanks for your help. Please continue. *A bientôt.*"

Gisèle had been in the resistance movement during the war. She had saved many people. And now she was going to save us!

Often she would tell us, when we looked at the photographs:

"Soon, they will be our leaders.

Soon they will be your fathers.

Soon they will be your family."

I was not sure just what she meant, but I knew it had to do with going to Palestine and having a Jewish homeland. All Gisèle wanted was to get all the children over there safely, past the blockades, past everyone who still didn't want us.

We, who never had papers.

Papers that said you could pass.

Papers that had the power.

One night I came down to the kitchen. It was dark and silent. Everyone slept. I saw a light in Gisèle's office and tiptoed to see who was there. She was sitting at her desk. The small lamp shed a pale and eerie light on her. She held her head in her two hands and wept.

I couldn't move. I didn't know what to do. Slowly, I approached, careful not to startle her. She seemed so far away. Her crying made me feel frightened. My world falling apart. I stood near, waiting. Hesitantly, I reached out and put my hand on her shoulder, hoping she'd let me in. Her strong arms encircled me.

"They didn't make it. The boat had to turn back. It was night. I was so sure they would get through. They must have been so frightened! They'll be held in Cyprus now. Another camp. Again. When will this end? Home, home. We must give all of you a home," she insisted, looking into space.

Sarah was on this convoy. My darling Sarah. My friend. Sarah, who waited until I was ready to speak. Sarah, who was the first, the only one, who made me answer when she had said that first night. "And now, tell me. You must tell me. What happened to you? Were you abandoned? Did you lose everyone? Were you left all alone? Have they all perished?"

Life went on. A gathering was being prepared to honor some of our benefactors. We were organizing varied performances, drawing from resources we didn't know we had in us. The stage would be in the garden. Chairs were being lined up. A phonograph too.

The sewing room became the focus of our fancies and imagination. "Hannah. Can I have a piece of red cloth?" Can I have a pink sash? Hannah, I need a belt. Hannah, can you sew this sheet so it looks like a toga? I am rehearsing tomorrow — please finish my turban!"

Requests were endless, excitement filled the air. We would recite. We would sing. We would dance. We would act. We would dream.

"Hannah," I said. "I need a piece of black cloth. No. Nothing else. Just a piece of black cloth. Thank you Hannah."

I cut it and sewed it into a small gathered skirt cut very short like a tunic. Then, I draped one long piece across my chest, leaving one shoulder bare and wrapping the rest around my waist. And that was all.

The music I chose was Chopin's *Marche Funèbre*. I came out barefoot, hair flowing loose, and started dancing.

I danced of the camps.
I danced of the suffering.
I danced of the dying.
I danced of the ones who would never come back.
I danced of the ones who would.
I danced of the emptiness.
I danced of the pain.
I danced of the loss.
I danced of the memories.

Gisèle rushed over and hugged me. She was crying. She was laughing.

"I just got the news from the last trip," she said. "They made it. They're in. I am so happy!" She lifted me up, her face full of smiles and tears. "And you," she said "will be next to go! Yes, You will be next!"

It is here
I should
have been.
Here
where I belong.

But,
how strange,
how new,
how alien,
it is.

For my soul,
my mind,
have been twisted
in so strange
a direction.

That no part
of me
is home,
here,
or
there.

And I
shall
forever
be left
to wander.

13

A
MAN
OF
LARGE
BLACK
EYES,
BURIED
DEEP
IN
THEIR
SOCKETS

My life
will begin
now.

I shall forget
the past.
And all
that came
before.

I will start
fresh.
Erase
the memory.

Freed
of all
I will be
as a newborn.

A clear
beginning
will help me
bear tomorrow.

He came unannounced.
  "I am here to take my children," he said.
  A man of skin and bones.
  A man of large black eyes, buried deep in their sockets.
  A man of bushy, snow-colored eyebrows.
  A man of sorrow.

He said "no" to everything.

"No. My wife isn't coming back.

No. I don't know what we shall do now.

No. I am not sure where we will live.

No. I don't want my children to go to Palestine.

No. I don't need your help. Thank you."

We packed two little bags. We said goodbye. We followed him. Our father.

The train from Toulouse to Grenade-sur-Garonne takes an hour. We sat, looking into space, not speaking. Papa stared out the window, his deep brown eyes buried deep in their cave, his mouth sunk between the hollow cheeks, the pointy chin bones piercing skin, the long oval face like half a moon in darkness. His bony left hand held a cigarette. Once in a while he inhaled the smoke. Papa was a ghost.

It was the end of April 1945. We were due to leave for Palestine on the next trip. Yvonne still had doubts. Gisèle had been trying to convince her.

Well, now it was all over. She didn't have to decide. Papa had returned, unexpectedly, and now he was taking us back to the village.

Jean had come upstairs to look for me earlier that day. Yvonne had been notified by Gisèle.

"Come, sit down," Jean had said. "I want to talk to you. What would you say if your father came back and wanted to take you home?" he gently asked.

"Jean," I replied, feeling suddenly flushed and upset, "don't tease me. I don't want to talk about those things. Why do you speak to me about my father? You know I'll never see him again."

"Do you remember him?" Jean asked.

"It's been more than two years, but I remember him. I see him every day," I said, reaching for the box. "I'll show you." I handed Jean the picture, pointing to Papa. "Look at him!" I said with pride. "How can you forget my Papa's face?"

Jean stared, and I saw his eyes open wide. A shiver went through his body. He looked very angry suddenly.

"That can't be your father!" he shouted.

"Well it is. Why do you think I would lie to you?" I asked, suddenly puzzled by his strange behavior.

Jean leaned over and hugged me tight. "I like you — I liked you from the first time I picked you up at the convent. Will you promise me something?"

"Yes. Anything. I like you too Jean, even though you scared me at first!"

"Promise you'll try to be happy no matter what happens. Even if you are not sure at first. It will turn out in the end. Can you promise me that?" he asked, looking straight into my eyes, waiting for an answer.

"Are you worried we'll get caught on the boat to Palestine and kept imprisoned in Cyprus?" I asked. "If we do, I'll see Sarah. I don't care. You don't have to think about it. I can take it. I just hope Yvonne will come. I don't know if I could leave without her," I added, getting sad just thinking she might decide not to go. She visited the convent regularly and took me to Mass with her on Sundays. I didn't think she would be able to separate from the nuns and the convent.

"No, I wasn't thinking of that," Jean said. "I was thinking that if something different happened. Like one of your parents returned — but it wouldn't be the same because the suffering they endured would make the person so different you wouldn't know them anymore. Like you'd be the grown up now. Like you couldn't expect the person to be in charge anymore. Like it would never be the same as it used to be — here," and Jean pointed to the picture.

"You mean like Hélène, whose mother returned, but is so ill she is dying in the hospital now, because they tortured her in the camps?" I said, trying to clarify what Jean was trying to tell me.

"Well, maybe not like that. Maybe in some other way. I don't know," he mumbled.

Jean looked confused. I was not used to that. He'd always seemed so sure of himself. Suddenly, I wanted to reassure him, comfort him. I didn't want to see him worried. In a loud voice I started to blurt out, sure I'd found the way.

"Do you remember when I first came here and the boiler broke, and only ice water came from the showers?" I asked, suddenly confident I could calm his fears.

"Yes — and so?" Jean questioned, his eyes fixed on the wall, his hands rubbing the knuckles one against the other.

"Well. No one wanted to wash, but I ran under the icy water, urging them to join in. Look I told them, as the icy water hit my body, I have no skin. I feel no pain. I suffer nothing. Cold does not touch me. Come and try it!" I'd told them.

But I knew, somewhere, buried inside, the hurt was hiding. Ice does not sting. Fire does not burn. If you cut, and find the heart, and open it, maybe? Maybe then? You'll touch. But no, not this. I feel no pain. Nothing.

"Remember? Jean. Well, that's how it is. I can promise you. Little will matter from now on. It will always be impossible for me, but I'll make the best of it." I've trained myself, I reassured him.

Jean looked at me. His kind eyes full of concern. His young face older, older than I had ever seen. His large hand came to rest on my head and slowly caressed the thick long dark hair, my secret treasure.

"Come with me, then," he'd said, in a stern voice I had never heard before.

I followed him to Gisèle's office. The door was closed. It was the first time I'd not seen it wide open. He knocked. "Come in," she said.

The strange grey man stood on one side. Gisèle and Yvonne opposite, holding on to the back of the desk, leaning against it.

My eyes opened wide.

"PAPA!
PAPA?
Is that you!
Is that really you?"

Is this my Father?
He
with hollow eyes
and
razor-thin face?

Did I recall
silver hair,
bones
soaring
through
parchment skin?

A slight gait,
hesitant walk,
pinched nostrils
not breathing
free.

Lips tightly shut
not parting
to smile?

Is this my Father?
Is it really
he?

14

I'LL
TRY
TO
SAY
IT
IN
HIS
OWN
WORDS

Gisèle looked at us sadly. We sat across her desk. She had wanted to be alone with us before we left the Château. She had asked Papa if it was all right. Papa said yes.

Jean led him to the garden. He pulled over two chairs. They sat facing each other. Papa held his hands together resting on his knees, his gaze fixed on the leaves of the nearby tree. Was Papa really there? Jean kept moving, crossing his legs from one side to the other. He seemed nervous. He tried talking, but Papa did not reply or look at him. "He is still in shock," Gisele remarked, as she stared at him through the window. "You must give him time, you must be patient."

She continued: "He told me General Patton found some survivors in the camp of Buchenwald where your father was for the last few months. He made a detour while advancing through Germany because he had heard a rumor there was a camp nearby, and he decided to see if there was anyone left alive. The SS were shooting everyone, but they didn't have time to complete the job."

She wanted to tell us what he had related to her, but she seemed lost, turning uncomfortably in her chair, glancing at Papa with sadness, shaking her head, holding back tears.

"I'll try to say it in his own words. It's hard for me to find a way to describe what he told me," she whispered with a sigh. "He's been in a few camps throughout the years. He only briefly told me about the last one and how he was transferred there. This is how your father explained it," she finally said.

(From the writings of my father done upon his return from camp in 1945 after liberation.)

"Before Buchenwald I was in camp at Gleiwitz in Poland, for a while. We learned that the Russians had launched their offensive at Baranow and our benefactors, who guard us so faithfully, now go forward, and not backward. We were quietly jubilant, but this was not yet the end

of our suffering. We must drink the cup of sorrow to the bitter end.

On January 16, 1945 all camps in this region are evacuated. We stupidly thought that we would be left there and were getting ready to welcome the Russians as our liberators. Far from it, however! What an irony of fate! Hitler wanted to make Germany "Judenrein" (free of Jews) and now he was bringing Jews to Germany. Our camp is also being evacuated. It is winter and we are scantily dressed. The camp commander tells us that we will have to walk for six days. He warns us that those who cannot keep up will be simply liquidated. The veterinary will remove the corpses.

And so we start. We have been walking for two days, spending the nights in barns, but the Russians march faster. They are everywhere except where we are. We turn back to Gleiwitz where we are loaded onto open cattle cars, 130-150 men per car. Only one direction is still open, towards Czechoslovakia. The train starts moving. If I now try to describe our journey, I feel, even today, as if I am going out of my mind. We have hardly room to stand, and if someone tries to sit down, he is done for. The train travels slowly and some of us are trying to jump down but the SS watch and those who try are shot on the spot. We travel for days and nights and the voyage is endless.

In each car there are many corpses. People die from thirst, hunger, the cold. Some go mad. We want to push the corpses out of the car, because the corpses are everywhere. We stand, kneel, walk over corpses. We ourselves are not much more than corpses. We arrive in a city and we see that it is Pilsen. The train stops and we scream so loudly that the whole town comes running. The inhabitants want to help us. They are trying to throw food into the cars because we are in Czechoslovakia, but the SS do not allow it, they shoot. We should simply drop dead.

The journey lasted seven days and seven nights and eventually we reached Buchenwald.

In Buchenwald there was the big camp and the small one. The latter was for us. It consisted of miserable wooden barracks with bare bunks, no straw, no blankets. Up to 1500 men were pushed into one barrack. There we were supposed to die a slow death. We did not have to work, because our work did not serve any purpose any more. We got so little food that many starved to death.

In the morning when we were carrying the corpses from the barrack, many lacked parts of their bodies. Hunger was stronger than any other feeling. We were like tigers devouring each other.

In February 1945, over 4000 corpses were removed from the small camp. Buchenwald did not have a gas chamber. There was a small crematory, though, but it could not manage this heavy press.

That was quite different from Birkenau the concentration camp where I had been before being transferred to Gleiwitz. When the last action against Jews began in Hungary, so many Jews were brought to Birkenau that even the huge crematories there could not keep up. The victims were gassed and then burned on open stakes. The inhabitants of the city of Auschwitz complained in Berlin that the stench from the Jewish flesh was unbearable.

Now we expect our end any day, because we know that there is no way out. In Buchenwald there were loudspeakers everywhere over which the orders of the SS administration were announced.

On April 8, 1945 we hear the following announcement:

"All Jewish inmates must report immediately to the assembly place."

We know what that means. We know that this is the end for us. The loudspeaker drones on: "Within an hour all Jews are to assemble. The "Blockälteste" and the "Lagerschutz" are responsible for the prompt execution of the order. IT IS URGENT!"

We are desperate. We do not want to die, just now when our liberators are so close. We hear the bombardment of Erfurt which is only seventeen kilometers from Buchenwald.

The hour goes by and no one has gone to the assembly place. This dreadful order is ignored by everyone because the Aryan inmates know that after us it will be their turn.

And again we hear the loudspeakers. This time it is a different tune: "Why did the Jews not assemble? In half an hour the Jews must be ready to march, otherwise the SS will come into the camp."

And, indeed, they invade the camp, armed with pistols they chase the miserable group to the assembly place. Shots are fired and some of us will not live to see the day of liberation. I manage to slip into an Aryan barrack. I must admit that some of us managed to save ourselves this way but, unfortunately, not everybody was so lucky.

The group of inmates the SS assembled is transported to Weimar but not any farther because the glorious "Wehrmacht" (armed forces) need every open road for a glorious retreat. What should one do with the Jewish scum?

The famous forest of Thuringia is not far from here. It is here where Goethe and Schiller lived, and it is here that the Jews were speedily liquidated. The whole group was shot down with machine guns. When four days later the inhabitants of Weimar were carrying the corpses back to Buchenwald, many a German woman fainted. On April 11, 1945 we were liberated. General Patton's tank spearheads opened the gates to freedom for us. Twelve days later I was in Paris."

(Original writings in Photo/Document section)

    Gisèle stopped talking. Her face was a gray color. She looked drained. Yvonne and I looked at each other. We were horrified. What were we going to do? How was Papa going to be now? He didn't look like the same man he once was. Perhaps he'd never be Papa again.

    Yvonne sat erect in the chair. I noticed her neck was twitching. I felt my body shaking, as if I had a fever. I wanted to run out to Papa, throw myself at his feet, beg him, implore: "Please Papa, be you again! Be you like before!" But I did not move, I waited for Yvonne.

"And then what did he do when he left the camp?" she asked.

Gisèle did not look as though she could continue. She hit her desk with the palm of her hand in a helpless gesture.

"Please!" Yvonne insisted.

Gisèle continued with my father's story. "The Americans" he said, "gave us clothes and food and organized to care for the sick and dying before sending us home. I walked into the nearest town and saw a car with the key in the ignition. I don't know whose it was. I went in and drove away. I couldn't stay there one more day. I saw a woman from a nearby camp walking on the road without shoes. I gave her a ride. We drove until the gas tank was empty. Then we stopped soldiers for food and lifts until we reached the French border.

The woman, Lela, went to look for her husband, her children, her parents. I went to search for my daughters and my mother. My wife is dead. I heard through some others who saw her in Auschwitz. She was in the medical experiment bloc 10 run by Dr. Mengele. They killed her."

"I didn't want to question him too much," Gisèle told us. "I just let him talk as much as he wanted. He is so weak and emaciated. I don't think he should be walking around. Every word he speaks is such an effort and he coughs until all his strength is gone. I think he should be hospitalized. I tried to offer help, but he refuses. He wants you to accompany him back to the village of Grenade. He says your grandmother will take care of you. I said I didn't think she could, that she was too old, but he wouldn't hear of anything else. I have no legal right to keep you here against his will, even though I know it would be to everyone's best interest right now."

Gisèle looked very concerned. Yvonne walked over to her, held out her hand, and firmly grasped Gisèle's wrist.

"Thank you for everything. I'll take care of him. Don't worry. And of her too," she said, pointing in my direction. "We'll keep you informed. I'll get our things and we'll leave with him. He probably thought we were all dead, just as we did. He can't wait now. Even though we are strangers, we'll have to get to know one another again."

I knew Gisèle was going to cry. She was trying hard to hold back her tears, but her face looked distorted, like when the wind blows and you try to look ahead with eyes half closed and all other parts locked tight to protect yourself.

"Come," Yvonne said, pulling me from the chair. My legs felt wobbly.

"Go upstairs and pack your bag. Don't forget to take your catechism. I'll notify mother Marie-Thérèse that we won't be coming to Mass Sunday at the convent." We had been going regularly.

"We'll have to go to the church in Grenade for the moment. And then we'll see," she added with a puzzled expression.

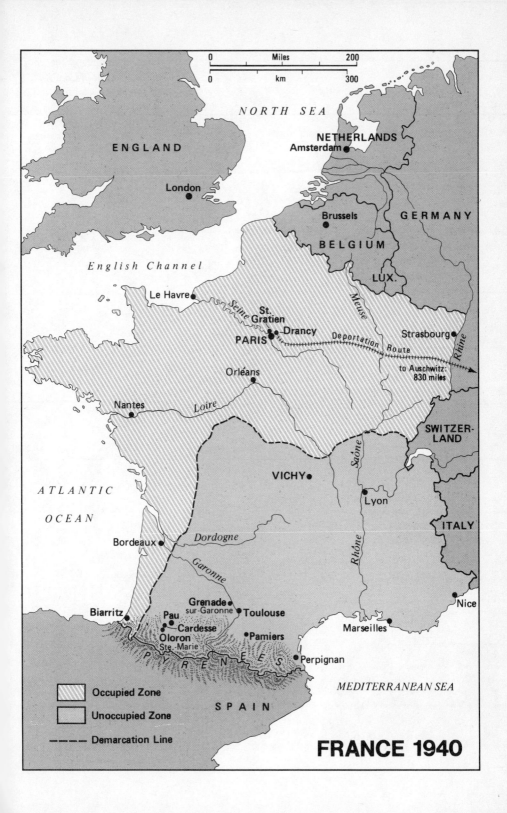

Miles 0 200
km 0 300

NORTH SEA

ENGLAND

NETHERLANDS
Amsterdam

London

GERMANY

Brussels

English Channel

BELGIUM

LUX.

Meuse

Le Havre

Seine

St. Gratien
Drancy

PARIS

Deportation Route

Strasbourg

Rhine

to Auschwitz: 830 miles

Orléans

SWITZER-LAND

Nantes

Loire

ATLANTIC OCEAN

VICHY

Saône

Lyon

ITALY

Bordeaux

Dordogne

Garonne

Rhône

Grenade sur-Garonne
Toulouse

Nice

Biarritz

Pau

Cardesse

Oloron Ste.-Marie

Pamiers

Marseilles

P Y R E N E E S

Perpignan

MEDITERRANEAN SEA

Occupied Zone

Unoccupied Zone

Demarcation Line

SPAIN

FRANCE 1940

et les religieuses franciscaines
nous entourerons nos deux chères enfants
nous dégageons à l'avance leur
responsabilité pour les accidents
qui pourraient survenir

Toulouse le 3 octobre 1942.

M. Fersztenfeld

F. Fersztenfeld

Letter of pledge signed by Maurice and Annette Ferstenfeld to the chaplain of the Franciscan Convent in Toulouse, October 3, 1942. It authorizes the children to be converted, and entrusts them to the care of the nuns. (Translation on Pages 95 & 96.)

Nous: Fersztenfeld Maurice et Fersztenfeld Hana, soussignés
déclarons confier nos deux enfants
1) Yvonne et Renée au Père Ange Bacquet, aumônier du
Monastère des franciscaines ou Port Saint Sauveur à Toulouse
pour qu'elles achèvent leur education dans cette maison.
Nous autorisons nos deux enfants
à se faire instruire de la religion
Chrétienne et à recevoir le
baptême si elles en expriment
librement le désir.
Nous nous engageons à ne rien
faire par la suite pour les
détourner de l'observance de
ladite Religion.
Confiants dans la solli-
citude dont le Père aumônier

Maurice just prior to this period.

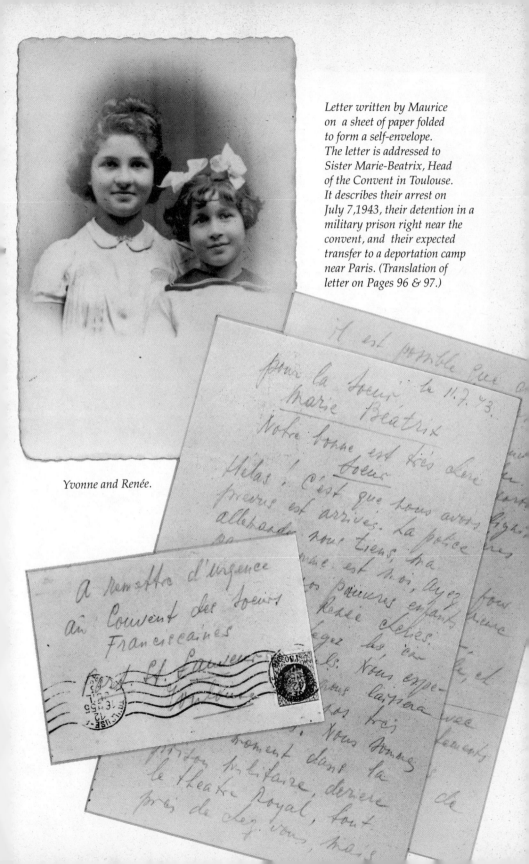

Letter written by Maurice on a sheet of paper folded to form a self-envelope. The letter is addressed to Sister Marie-Beatrix, Head of the Convent in Toulouse. It describes their arrest on July 7,1943, their detention in a military prison right near the convent, and their expected transfer to a deportation camp near Paris. (Translation of letter on Pages 96 & 97.)

Yvonne and Renée.

Letter sent by B. Jacques from Drancy, in which he explains that he picked up a note scrawled on a small piece of cardboard. The note was thrown by Maurice, from a truck that was transporting him and other Jews from the Drancy Camp. It was addressed to a Mr. Kessler of Grenade-sur-Garonne, informing him of their deportation to Poland. (Translations of letter and note on Page 120.)

P. AGATHANGE
Couvent des Capucins
CÔTE-PAVÉE - Toulouse
Mercredi-Samedi-Dimanche
de 13 h à 16 h.
33, Côte-Pavée, TOULOUSE (H.-G.)

PROCURE DES MISSIONS

Toulouse le 31 octobre 1945.

Ma chère Enfant,

Vous me demandez un...
gieuse qui doit vous accueil...
ers et ce sera la présente l...
de la main de vos chers pare...
sur eux, pour vous avoir ens...
au baptême et préservée de...
1943-44, je puis, mieux que...
votre force d'âme, de...
furent votre...

votre vi...

Toulouse le 8 mai.

Ma Chère Enfant,

Ma paternité, pour être
spirituelle, reste toujours en souci
pour vous. aussi vos nouvelles me
tout-elle...

PROCURE DES MISSIONS
OUBANGHI-CHARI...
...FRANÇAISE...

DIOCÈSE DE TOULOUSE — PAROISSE DE SAINT-ÉTIENNE

Extrait du Registre des Actes de Baptême

L'an mil neuf cent quarante-trois le sept du mois de mars
a été baptisée par nous, soussigné, Marie Yvonne Marguerite
Née le 9 mai 1929 fille de M. Maurice FERSTENFEL...
D. Anne Parzer... mariés.

...1945

DIOCÈSE DE TOULOUSE — PAROISSE DE SAINT-ÉTIENNE

NOTE MARGINALE

Extrait du Registre des Actes de Baptême

L'an mil neuf cent quarante-trois le sept du mois de mars
a été baptisée par nous, soussigné, Marie Renée Françoise Thérèse
Née le 31 janvier 1934 fille de M. Maurice FERSTENFELD
et de D. Anne Parzer mariés.
Parrain, M. Marcel Svigre
marraine, D. Léonie Huron
qui ont signé avec le R.P. Agathange délégué
certifié conforme,
Toulouse le 22 octobre 1945.

6. Le Curé.
P. Fouqui...

Letters written by Father Agathange after the war to Yvonne and Renée, saying his prayers and wishes are always with them. He enclosed copies of their Baptismal Certificates. The Baptism took place on March 7, 1943 in Toulouse. Yvonne was renamed Marie-Yvonne-Marguerite, and Renée was renamed Marie-Renée Françoise Thérèse.

Ryd le 4.6.45

Mes très chers petites filles.
J'ai de nouveau une occasion de
vous envoyer une lettre qui
serra emporté en Avion et mise
en boîte a Paris donc ca ira plus
vite j'ai déja écrit maint fois
et jamais de réponse.
Comment allez vous je suis très
inquiette a votre sujet est pense
jour et nuit a vous, si seul-
ment je pouvait avoir un
mot de vous, vois votre cher
écriture avoir un Photo de vous,
cela me ferait t...

(Left) One of the letters written by Annette from Sweden, where she was in rehabilitation after being liberated by the Red Cross. (Translation of letters on Pages 245 to 248.) (Photo of Annette during this period.)

(Above) Some pages from Maurice's writings, and a photo of him during this period. (Translations of excerpts from Maurice's writings on Pages 137 to 140, 168 to 181, 194 to 200 and 220 to 224.)

Convoy 57, July 18, 1943

There was no Convoy 56, on June 24, 1943, contrary to the Rut
file, containing 450 names, is only a projected convoy. Examina
shows that they left for Auschwitz in later convoys or were no
again, the Auschwitz calendar believed that the deportees of this p
all gassed, since no trace of them could be found. The report on
tion of Drancy (CCXXI-19; quoted in Convoy 55) probably would have
of June 24 had there been one, since it specifically mentioned the

Document CCXXI-19 describes Convoy 57 as "deportation to
internees, among them many French in origin, and a large number ...
dren." A note of July 17 (DLXII-26) describes the organization o
the convoy.

This was the first routine telex to Eichmann and Auschwitz
the great m...

ENGHIEN	06.05.05	EZZAOUI	SIM...	from	...ourget/Drancy
	12.08.98	MINSK	EZZAOUI	SULTA...	...not Roth...
HENRI	25.11.18	LYDA	FABRICANT	ANNA	05.03.88
...E	25.02.26		FABRICANT	DAVID	01.09.85
...TE	19.09.86		FALLER	PIERRE	19.05.81
	13.03.22		FANTO	OLGA	19.11.95
	13.05.82		FARBERT	CHARLES	21.03.85
...T	12.12.92	ROUBAIX	FARBSTEIN	DAVID	09.09.77
...E	02.07.93	PARIS	FAYERSTEIN	DYNA	03.09.19 VARSOVIE
	09.01.86	PARIS	FDIDA	SIMON	03.06.16
	29.10.95	PARIS	FEDER	HENRI	01.01.32
	28.01.22	PARIS	FEDER	MICHEL	04.03.97
	06.01.31	PARIS	FEDER	LAJA	26.02.39
	05.08.02	ROUEN	FEDER	LAJA	14.05.04
	18.10.15	PARIS	FEDER	LEON	24.09.36
...M	14.02.24		FEDER	RACHEL	06.09.42
...RINE	24.03.08		FEDER	SALOMON	08.01.29
	17.09.11		FEDER	SOPHIE	02.07.34
...ES	08.04.09	PARIS	FEHR	MARGUERITE	07.04.84
	09.08.26	PARIS	FEIGIN	FRANIA	23.09.96
...NE	31.12.14	ALGER	FELDMANN	BEREK	01.01.74
...EINE	28.12.10	BIALISTOCK	FELDSTEIN	ALBERT	20.08.19
	10.07.07		FELIX	MARCELLE	19.01.06
	07.02.02	RADOM	FELMAN	ISRAEL	13.12.84
...S	24.08.25		FERSZTENFELD	ANNA	07.08.05
...TE	08.02.92	PARIS	FERSZTENFELD	MOISE	07.03.05
	03.04.07	KICHINEFF	FINKEL	ISHOUDA	24.02.00
...ES	29.01.10		FINKIELSTEIN	HENRI	19.10.26
...EL	.84	SALONIQUE	FINKIELSTEIN	JOSEPH	31.12.30 PARIS
...I	01.06.25		FINKIELSTEIN	SZANDLA	10.10.88 VARSOVIE
	03.06.31		FISZBIN	DAVID	18.10.99 BIALISTOCK
...TH	.07	BEYROUTH	FLESIG	MONIQUE	07.05.22
...ICE	08.09.19	ORAN	FOGELNEST	RUBIN	19.01.06
...E	.06		FOURMANN	DAVID	16.08.13 PARIS
	.79	ALGER	FRAENKEL	LEON	22.01.87 PARIS
...AIN	23.01.16		FRANCES	JACOB	11.11.14 SALONIQUE
	10.02.82		FRANCFORT	BERTHE	16.02.79 PARIS
...NE	22.04.85	ASNIERES	FRANCFORT	GERMAINE	13.06.02 PARIS
...NIE	01.12.97		FRANCFORT	HENRI	13.07.69 PARIS
...ENNE	31.01.20		FRANCFORT	PAULETTE	19.03.33 PARIS
...ON	17.01.17	LE CAIRE	FRANCFORT	PIERRE	28.04.29 PARIS
...RD	13.09.01		FRANCFORT	ROGER	16.02.02 PARIS
...E	23.12.01				17.0...78 JASSY
...NTN	17....				ROUEN
	01				

...shed open and nightmarish m...enc... e...
people, in striped clothes, jump on the train, like gno...
escaped from hell. Behind them, the SS, rifles pointin...
crying: 'Los, raus, alles raus, Los' (Fast, outsid...

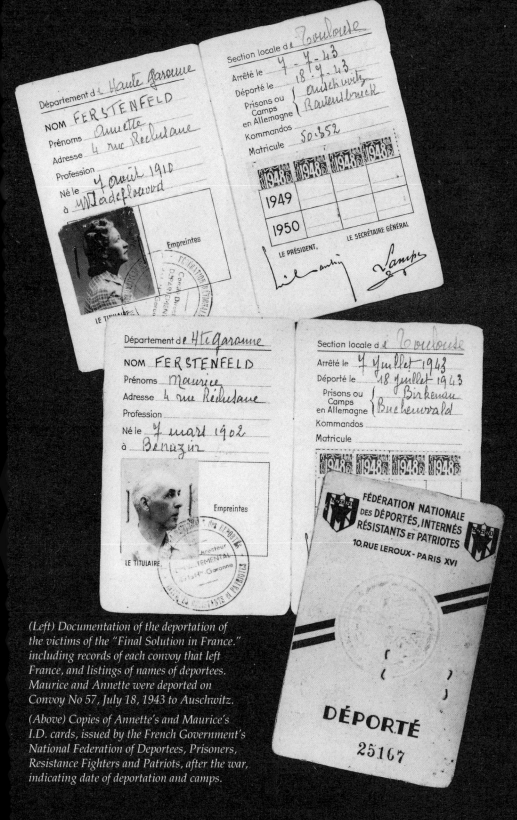

(Left) Documentation of the deportation of the victims of the "Final Solution in France," including records of each convoy that left France, and listings of names of deportees. Maurice and Annette were deported on Convoy No 57, July 18, 1943 to Auschwitz.

(Above) Copies of Annette's and Maurice's I.D. cards, issued by the French Government's National Federation of Deportees, Prisoners, Resistance Fighters and Patriots, after the war, indicating date of deportation and camps.

(Left and Below)
Annette and Maurice
in their twenties.

Yvonne age seven,
and Renée age two,
in Paris.

THE
EARLY
YEARS

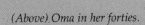

(Above) Oma in her forties.

(Left) Yvonne, Renée and Mirka
in St. Gratien, in front of the garden,
before leaving on the exodus south
to Free France at the beginning
of the war.

(Below) Renée, age one, in Paris.

(Above and Below) Maurice in Toulouse after the war.

(Right) Annette and Aunt Méry taking a stroll in Toulouse.

(Right) Yvonne and Renée in front of the house in Grenade. Photo was taken in 1942, just before being sent into hiding in the Franciscan convent of Toulouse.

Oma after the war.

(Above) Annette and Nanita in Grenade, on their daily walk to the Garonne river.

(Left) Portrait of Yvonne and Renée in Grenade, after the war.

(Below) Yvonne, Oma, Maurice and Renée in Grenade, just after Papa's return.

PHOTOS TAKEN CIRCA 1940-45

(Above) Portrait of Annette, Maurice, Yvonne and Renée, in Toulouse.

(Left) Portrait of Renée after the war.

(Top Right-clockwise) Cousin Armand, Yvonne and Renée in Grenade when family came to visit after the war.

Cousin Irène and Renée, on the same day.

(Middle) Aunt Méry, Maurice and Annette, in Toulouse.

(Bottom) Yvonne and Renée in Toulouse while still living in the orphanage, Le Château.

Maurice and Annette in a cafe in Toulouse.

*(Top) Maurice and Annette enjoying
a bottle of wine, in Paris.*

*(Right) Yvonne and Renée. All grown up now...
and living in America.*

*(Bottom) Renée's family today. Husband Bernard,
daughter Caren, son Marc and Renée, at home.*

15

THE
ROAD
TO
MY
HOME
IS
ENDLESS

The road to my home
is endless.
I've lost it
a thousand times.

From left
to right.
From North
to South.

Each turn
a resting place.
But nowhere
is my home.

Forever
gone.

The wheels moved noisily along the track. The train is slow, straining like an old tired man.

The distance from Toulouse to Grenade is only about twenty kilometers, but there are frequent stops along the way — sometimes at a small village station where someone gets on or off, sometimes simply to wait while another train passes in the opposite direction or for some other reason unknown to the passengers.

I feel strange about being on this train again. It reminds me of all the trips we had made with Maman. First leaving to enter the convent. Then returning home on holidays. Finally taking it for the last time, going back to the convent after Papa and Maman were arrested and taken away on the truck by the Germans.

"They're alone now. They're orphans now," they whispered around us, as we stood watching the truck's outline dim in the distance. New words opening a world of terror, of unknown walks through a dark forest. Words I never knew before — *alone, orphans*.

Where is the train taking us now?

Through the glass window the beautiful countryside seems untouched. The cows graze peacefully as though nothing had happened, their big bulging eyes stare at us as we pass by.

"Don't they know the world stopped breathing?"

Spring is almost in the air. The red, white and blue wild flowers start to push the ground, along the way, wherever a piece of uncultivated earth welcomes them.

The *marguerites*, the *bleuets*, and the *coquelicots*. Our national country flowers. The colors of our flag. The subject of so many songs and poems. The inspiration of our most famous painters.

"Don't they know the world stopped breathing?"

Next to us other passengers are laughing, cutting big chunks of light brown bread and fragrant salamis full of garlic. They are opening bottles of deep red wine. *A votre santé! A votre santé!* They toast, hitting their glasses against each other with loud clicking sounds.

Their faces are ruddy, their eyes shine from the warmth of the brew. The war is over. They're free again. The straw baskets they have taken on board the train for lunch are bulging. Next comes out a runny camembert, some juicy fruits.

"Do you want one?" the kind lady asks. She smiles, hand outstretched with her offering.

"*Non, merci Madame,*"I say.

"Don't they know the world stopped breathing?"

As for the three of us, we have nothing to talk about. Nothing to say to each other. Not yet.

I think of the church, our new faith. After all, can I deny that our secret mission worked? That it bore fruit? Not completely, as we asked for, but still, in part. Will that make me a stronger believer? Did Yvonne see things I did not? I had always thought our scheme would work. That God would see Papa and Maman's faces and search them out, since he could watch the whole world from where he was.

As time went on I had wanted to forget the special offering we had made to God to save them. It was hard to admit we had failed. That God had not paid close attention. That we had been duped, so to say. It all came back to me now, as I glanced at Papa from the corner of my eyes.

I still feel the shadow of that terrible room. The stench of Sister Marie-Valentine's decomposing body. The dark aura that surrounded her form, somberly clad in the black habit. The waxen face, like a huge oval stone, centering the immaculate white coif. I had asked so much of her in my prayers. She was a saint, and her soul was in heaven. I was sure she could help.

It was the night after we visited Sister Marie-Valentine on her death bed that I had this dream. She was lying in the little room in back of the chapel, while we filed by to say goodbye and ask her to grant wishes. She was with God now, and could tell him first hand. As I spoke to her she opened her eyes.

"Put the picture under the altar during Sunday Mass," she told me. "God will find your father, mother and grandmother, and will reunite your family."

Then, she closed her eyes and didn't speak to me anymore. I wanted her to repeat what she had said. I wanted to be sure I had heard correctly, but she didn't. I took her hand and started to pull it, begging her to wake up once more and talk to me again.

Then, I woke up.
It was a dream.
A dream!
If only it were true!
She had come to talk to me.
She had told me what to do.
I was trembling.

She had been near me,
brushed against my breath.
She had whispered the way.
I would not doubt her word.

It was pitch black in the dormitory. I put my bare feet on the cold wooden floor and crouched beneath the bed.

Should I pray? Should I thank Sister Marie-Valentine?

I slid my hand under the mattress. I felt the box. Slowly I pulled it out and opened it. It was too dark to see, but I knew where everyone was in the picture, so it didn't really matter. My fingers glided from Papa's head to Maman's. I caressed Oma's hand.

"I am going to do what Sister Marie-Valentine said!" I told them. "I'll talk to Yvonne, and she will ask Mother Superior, and Sunday you will go to Mass with us. God will find each of you and reunite us all together!"

My eyes got used to the darkness now. Some moon shone through giving me a bit of light. The sun would rise soon and we would have to get up. I quickly closed the box and hid it back in its place.

"Soon," I told them.

"Soon I will take you to the chapel.

Soon God will find everyone of you,

wherever you are,

and then, we'll be together again.

Sister Marie-Valentine is a saint.

She won't let me down.

She opened her eyes and told me what to do,

and I will.

Soon, we'll be together.

Once more,

just like before."

I closed my eyes. Happiness flowing warmly around me like a caress.

"Maman,
when you find me,
will you buy me back?"
I had asked, as I drifted into sleep.

Next day I told Yvonne about the dream. I asked if she would speak to Mother Superior for permission to put the picture under the altar for Sunday Mass. She said she would, that it might help, especially if we gave secret offerings to God, said prayers and made private sacrifices.

We had brought the picture to Mass a number of times.

"God will hear you my children. Have faith. You must believe," Mother Superior said, as she hid the photo under the altar's white lace covering just before services were to start.

We said special prayers and made extra sacrifices. God looks and rewards the penitent. I was convinced. Why did God only see Papa and not Maman? I wonder, as I look at his strange shrunken face.

"Oh! You ungrateful, unbelieving sinner," I silently blame myself now. "Even in confession and repentant prayers I will not be forgiven for my greed, my lack of thankfulness. If God has granted our wish in part only, is that not enough to prove his eternal grace?"

But in my heart I am not satisfied. Something went wrong. We did everything we could. Gave up the smallest pleasures. Prayed to the point of exhaustion.

"Did you not hear us God? I thought all voices reached your almighty being? Where is my Maman God? Where is she?"

All around us the passengers are gathering their bags. We must be approaching Grenade.

"Come on," Yvonne says. "Stop dreaming and give me a hand, we're getting off soon." She handed me the bag.

They were waiting at the small station. It was just a narrow parapet with a bench underneath.

I see Oma, golden Oma. So old. So noble. So proud. Standing near her is Nanita, Maman's friend. The woman who calls herself our Godmother, claiming a little ownership, now that Maman is gone. Next to Nanita is Francis, her large-framed, red-haired husband, whom we call Parrain, the endearing term for God-father. And there are a few people I don't recognize — curiosity seekers, perhaps — coming to watch the reunion of lost souls.

Oma looks like a lioness. Her bushy silver hair all tied into a knot in back of her head. Her piercing black eyes sharp like the wind.

"I knew it would be this way. I knew we'd be together again some day," she whispers, not finding the strength to speak out loud, so shaken was she to see us reappear in her life.

Nanita holds a package. She hands it to me and takes me in her arms, crying and laughing at the same time.

"It's a dress. I made it in your favorite color. It's all embroidered with bee's nests. It has a wide sash. Sunday you must wear it. I'll make ice cream for you. We'll pick fresh berries." She is shaking, not fully coherent.

Parrain grabs his bicycle. "Come on, jump in back, skinny," he says. We'll take you home.

Papa is silent. Papa is tired. Papa can't feel happy.

We go through the narrow streets of the sleepy village. Some shutters are open. Old wrinkled faces greet us, waving the procession on.

The house stands at the corner looking the same, as though no time had passed, as though nothing had changed.

"We can stay here safely now," I hear. "They can no longer come to hurt us. We won. We won the war."

The wooden front door opens and I see the narrow passage to the back room we had shared with Oma. And I see the first room, where Papa and Maman used to stay, where we cooked, where we ate.

Two years. An eternity. Things remain. Stones. Dirt floors. Rooms. But we, we are no more. We've been destroyed. These walls should be for others. Others who have lost nothing. Others who are new. Who have no memories. No yesterdays.

"Take your place as before," Yvonne says, and I follow. "Put your catechism under the mattress," she orders, and I do. "You are not to tell Oma we are going to remain Catholic." I nod obediently. "Tomorrow morning we will go to early Mass. We'll leave through the window so they don't hear. We'll be back before they are up. You understand?"

"Yes. I know. We must be grateful. We must go to Mass. We must not sin. We must give confession. We must take communion. But Oma must not know about it. I'll do whatever you say." I whisper.

And I remember that day, when we first placed the photo under the altar, and the promise I had made to God, which I knew helped return Papa to us. No. I would never forget my promise.

Who am I now?
A strange being
with two heads
and no heart.
Dismembered,
empty.
Looking for yesterday.
A day
that will never return.

16

"THERE, THERE, EVERYTHING WILL BE FINE!"

The next morning I heard Papa say sadly to Oma, "what will we live on?"

Oma had hidden on a farm during the years we were gone. She had closed the house and left. She knew the Germans would come back for her too. She didn't want to stay there alone.

Oma looked at Papa, with a twinkle in her eyes. "Come," she said.

She took a small shovel in one hand, a rag in the other. We followed her, around the empty well, to a deserted corner of the small wall-enclosed garden. She bent, planting her crackling knees firmly in the soft ground. She started digging a hole, then moved to the left a bit, and looked around to be sure she was in the right place before she continued.

"Can we help you Oma?" we asked, not sure of what she was up to.

"No. I'll take care. Just give me time. Let me look around a minute!"

Some old cages were still stacked against one wall, but they were empty. No more rabbits, chickens, geese. No wild cats running around. They had all left. Everything was gone. It would never be the same.

I looked in back at the shed. The throne Papa built years ago was still there. The throne, Kuku. My head felt heavy with memories, regrets, losses.

Just let it be as it was. Just once more. Please! I silently begged, as I closed my eyes. It was so sunny then. So happy. Every detail was clear in my mind, as though returning here could make it come alive once more.

They say a chicken is an animal. They say a chicken is not human. That may be true, but not for Kuku.

Kuku had been my pet, my lovely companion in those early

months in Grenade.

She gave me an egg, almost every day.

She gave me wonderful conversation.

She gave me a reason to run out in the morning and say hello!

At that time, no one was allowed to own unregistered animals. Cows, pigs, goats, horses, lambs were all carefully counted by the authorities. They belonged to our conquerors, the Germans, and you had no right to own them unless you were a farmer and accounted regularly for them. This applied to small animals also, but it was a little harder to control, so you could have some of those.

There were eight small cages piled one on top of the other against one stone wall of the small garden. Four chickens, two rabbits, two geese lived there.

The chickens were for egg laying. Every morning, I took a small basket and went to look for eggs. I'd stand on my tip toes and reached up to the highest cage looking through the mesh to see if something good had occurred. Then, I opened the latch and slowly started to feel around the cage for the little roundness that brought joy to my heart. The chickens did not like to relinquish their treasure. You had to reach under their behinds and give them a little push so you could get to the egg, which was still warm and moist under their loving care.

The cages below had the rabbits. They were sweet and I loved to look at their cute little ears and the long munching teeth in front that never stopped moving. I tried not to love them too much, because at times they disappeared, and there was a big to do the next day over a stew simmering slowly in the hearth.

The last two cages were for the geese. The geese were not here to lay eggs or make a stew. The geese were here to be force-fed with corn kernels. Papa would get them at the farm and when their livers got very big Papa would bring them back to the farmer and get two new skinny geese to do the same. For doing this Papa would always bring back something special to eat, like a ham or sausage, some goose fat or other good things.

I didn't know what a liver was and why they wanted big ones. I had heard big fat livers were special. With it, you could make goose liver pâté which was something very good sold in little tin cans. I always wondered how they got the liver out from the stomach of the goose and put it into the little tin can. Sometimes when the new skinny geese came to replace the others, I would ask: "Did you come to live with us before? Did they send you back to get another fat liver? I wish you would tell me how they put your other liver in the little tin can? Sure must be interesting!" The geese never told me.

Oma and I would prepare every day for their feeding. Oma had a wooden chair with a straw seat. I had a little stool next to her. We took a goose and put it between our knees, holding tight, then we placed a funnel gently into the goose's throat. We dropped a few kernels of corn into the funnel and pushed down with a little wooden pestle. It formed a little ball on the goose's neck. When the ball was large enough we put a little water in the funnel and then, with two fingers around the neck, we slowly pushed it down into the stomach in one long stroke. We did this a number of times.

How this connected to the fat liver and the little tin cans, I never found out. We did it every day until Papa said the geese were fat enough. That was not my favorite work. It certainly was not as nice as getting the milk from the little corky nipples of the cows on the farms where Papa would take me sometimes. That was much more fun.

After all animals were fed and the cages cleaned I ran to get Kuku's leash. "Come on, Kuku, let's go."

The little garden had a stone wall all around. There was a wooden door to come in and out. It was hard to reach and open the heavy latch, but Kuku patiently waited until I finished fussing with it and off we went, just the two of us.

One day Maman said we would have to take a nap because there would be work to do throughout the night. We were not told what it was, but Papa had disappeared, and when all was dark outside he came home carrying something very big in a blanket. The father of another family, also in hiding in Grenade, carried the other end. A long table was set up in the hallway, and by the light of candles we stared at this dead pig lying on the flat surface.

If we all worked hard there would be hams and sausages and delicious white rendered fat called *saindoux*, which you spread on bread as a great delicacy. The pig came from a farmer whose daughter Papa was tutoring. This was the payment. It had been raised on the side, not included in the count the farmers had to give periodically to the authorities.

We had to cut up the pig immediately so there would never be a trace of its existence. Big knives carved all around. Soon chunks and pieces were piled on the table. They were divided into categories and processed accordingly. My job turned out to be cleaning the entrails. You had to wash them in a big bucket of water and then cut them into equal pieces. Maman and Oma were making sausage filling by chopping the small pieces of meat that were left and mixing them with herbs and spices. We made a knot at one end of the entrails and pushed the filling in. When the sausage was filled up, we made a knot on the other side. As dawn came, the pig was gone, and there would be hearty food for a long time.

When we had first arrived in Grenade I asked Maman where to go for a *pipi*. She seemed puzzled, looked around at the two rooms, quickly realizing this house definitely did not provide a toilet. We went into the garden, looked again. Could we? Should we? Well, what else could we do? For the moment anyway.

The next morning we decided a solution had to be found. Going into the fields did not seem like a good idea. We inspected every corner in search of a suitable site. The barn, at the end of the garden, is what we settled on. It was private, out of the way. You could close the door and be alone.

Papa got a big shovel and dug an enormous hole. Then he got wooden planks, which we placed over the entire area, leaving an opening in the center. On this hole, he built a wooden seat. We cut some paper into little squares and stuck them on a long nail. Papa wasn't very handy with a hammer. It took some time to mount the throne — but, when it was finished, we all stood in awe at the ingenious achievement. Mostly, we were happy to have a place to go.

This was a very fine place. A place to reflect and be alone. Often we stood on line outside, waiting for our turn. The planks rattled a bit as you walked toward the throne, but once you got there, the kingdom was yours.

One day I was sitting and reflecting dreamily when Kuku walked in. I had let her out of her cage, as we were soon to leave on our walk.

"Hello Kuku," I said. "Come over and wait near me. We'll go soon." She started toward me, lifting her paws daintily. Suddenly, a plank gave way and jumped into the air to one side. Kuku lost her balance and fell in the hole. I knew I couldn't save her alone. I ran in the house screaming. "Help me, help me. Kuku fell in the throne room. Help!"

Papa, Maman, Oma, Yvonne all ran out. In minutes we surrounded the hole. Some of us leaned over the opening, urging Kuku to come close so we could grab her out. Others were helping Papa pull out some planks around the broken one, so we could have a better grasp on her. Kuku was wildly running and splashing us all over with the contents below. She was beside herself and would not listen. She seemed dazed. Even I, her closest friend, could not get through and stop her from flopping around and splashing all of us with the contents of the hole.

Finally Maman got a hold of Kuku. In horror we looked at her, and each other, realizing only a heavy rain could save us all. She hobbled over to me, dizzy and bewildered. Then, breathing hard, she lay down gently next to my feet.

"Oma, let's get a big bucket of water and wash Kuku together," I said.

"No. We can't." Oma replied. "She won't survive this. She will get sick. We'll have to kill her now so at least we'll get a meal out of her. If we wait, she'll get ill and we won't be able to use her once she's contaminated."

I looked around in horror. I could not believe this was happening. Oma and I had plucked many chickens together. We sat close, facing each other. She, on the wooden chair. I, on the little stool. Oma did the neck because it was more delicate. I would start at the feet. Quickly, one by one, we lifted a feather at a time and pulled it off in one quick stroke. We saved the feathers in a basket. When we had enough we would stuff a pillow with them.

When the chicken was all plucked, Oma took a candle and lit it. She held the chicken by the neck and feet and rotated it over the lit candle which I was holding. The flame singed off any remaining stubble and left the chicken's skin smooth all over. Oma and I checked it for perfection by going over the little body with our palms, looking for any area of resistance. I liked the smell of the burning process. It was strange and mysterious.

Oma usually cooked the chicken in a soup. We always saved the neck to stuff with flour, mixed with fat and spices. That was my favorite. I would oversee its preparation and help with the sewing of the neck on each end after the stuffing was completed. We used a long needle and thin string and ended up with a funny-looking package, long and skinny, bulging all over from its contents.

The horror of this happening to my beloved Kuku was overwhelming. I put my hand on her, listening to her little heart pounding loudly, and looked up to see if someone would act in our defense. It was obviously useless.

So long ago and the pain was still there. I came out of my reverie with a start, as I heard Oma's loud voice.

"Here! Here it is!" Oma exclaimed triumphantly as she dug out the square metal box. It took a few tries until she found the exact place, but she had finally succeeded. She handed the box to Papa. "Let's go in," he said.

Oma held on to his arm, wiping the box with her free hand, leaning over to him. Papa placed the box on the kitchen table. We all stood around as he carefully opened it. "Oh!" we exclaimed, as he slowly lifted the lid. "It's all there," Oma said proudly. "It's all there, just as you left it," she repeated, as we stood staring in disbelief.

A few stacks of bills neatly folded. Maman's jewelry, laid out in a separate small box, shining gold, glittering stones, smooth white pearls. At the bottom was a folder, filled with documents and various papers, official-looking with stamps and embossed photographs.

Papa turned to Oma and let her embrace him, as though he was a small child. He bent his silver head in her shoulder and sobbed. Oma gently caressed his back, rocking his body softly. "There, there, my beloved son," she whispered.

"Everything will be fine. Everything will be fine."

TESTIMONY

It was hard to talk to Papa. Impossible to make him laugh, or even smile. His eyes no longer looked like burning holes, now that we got used to them. But, still, it wasn't really Papa.

Oma did everything she could to make him better.

"Do whatever he wants. Don't ask anything. Be quiet. He is writing," she reminded us, lest we disturb his peace.

Oma took charge of the household with Yvonne, and they said I could help. Papa spent countless hours writing page after page, filling them with neat blue lines from his fountain pen. It seems he could only talk to the long narrow onion paper notebook. No one else understood his sorrow.

"What is he writing?" Yvonne asked Oma.

"I don't know," Oma answered. "I heard him mumble he is giving testimony. That the murderers must be punished. He won't tell me. Let's just leave him until he's done what he has to accomplish. Maybe he'll feel better then," Oma sadly added, with a worried look in her somber eyes.

One day, Yvonne whispered she wanted to do something important later. She asked me to go outside in the garden so we could talk. I followed her. Whatever she decided to do was good enough for me.

"We'll go in when he goes to sleep," she said in a low voice. "Then we'll see what he is writing about. Better take a rest in the day. Go look for some candles. We'll take the notebook to the barn and return it before he awakens."

"What if we can't find the notebook?" I asked. "What if Papa puts it away somewhere?" I felt this was a very daring thing to do. I was frightened.

"We'll see later. In the meantime just do as I ask," she replied with authority. Yvonne always knew what to do. Anyway, I wasn't going to argue with her. Just like that time with the chocolates — long ago when we lived in this house and I had gotten into trouble.

Maman used to come every night to our bed for a goodnight kiss, and she gave us a sweet chocolate bonbon. Yvonne had told me one night she had discovered where the box was kept and, when Oma was asleep, she would go and take out a few and no one would know. Yvonne had tiptoed to the corner in the back of the hallway. Inside the old trunk she found the box. She had removed a handful and gave me my share. Oh, how I trembled with excitement. I can still recall.

In the dark my dilemma grew. I didn't want to eat the chocolate. I felt bad because Maman wouldn't know about it. I didn't want to tell Yvonne. She'd tell me I was a baby. I was afraid to get up and put it back. It was so dark! So I decided to wait for the next day. I would put the chocolates under my pillow and return them when no one was around.

In the morning I lifted the pillow and found most bonbons had melted. I desperately scraped what was left and approached the trunk to replace them. Maman caught me, of course, and Oma found the melted mess as she was fixing my bed.

I got punished for taking the chocolates, and now I wasn't even going to get the one I normally got at night, for a whole week. Yvonne was mad too. She said I was a baby and could have gotten both of us in trouble if I had talked. What if we got caught now? What would happen?

What was Papa writing anyway? All these hours without stop. What would we find out there? Would we know more about what happened to him? And to Maman? Was he writing things he couldn't talk about? In any case I would do whatever Yvonne decided. There was no doubt about that.

Night came, and still Papa wrote and wrote, sitting at the small table. He had lit a candle instead of using the electric bulb. The dim light flickered near the page while his hand traveled back and forth. He often dipped the pen in the ink well, and the blue liquid etched the paper, making his words come alive.

Yvonne crouched near the door waiting. I was told to stay at the end of the hallway, carefully holding two candles and some matches. Oma was sleeping. Her faint snoring filled the silence beyond the back room door, which we had carefully shut.

"Well now they'll know!" we heard Papa say out loud in a weary voice. He blew on the candle and the smoke traveled out of the front room, making cloudy ringlets that slowly disintegrated in the hallway. Yvonne put a finger to her lips, indicating I should remain quiet. She told me to stay where I was.

We waited in the darkness until we heard Papa's breathing, heavy and regular, and we knew he had succumbed to sleep. Then Yvonne called me and we entered the room. Papa was fully dressed. He had just kicked off his shoes, and they were lying on the floor like two lost tiny boats in a big ocean. Papa was lying on his stomach, both arms outstretched, like a penitent.

Yvonne slowly gathered the loose pages of the notebook and carefully placed them between the covers of a book she had taken with her.

"Come on," she whispered, as she pulled me toward the door. I would have wanted to cover Papa. Kiss his cheek. Tell him I still loved him, even if he wasn't Papa anymore. Ease his pain, if he let me, but I was afraid to wake him, and Yvonne motioned me urgently before I did anything foolish.

We climbed up the ladder in the barn at the end of the garden, making a spot on the hay-covered balcony. The same one where we had played so many games. The same one where we had read fairy tales on hot lazy afternoons. The same one where Kuku and I hid from the world.

"Let's light the candle," Yvonne said.

The pale flame trembled as it illuminated the first page. The words looked like bruises, like twisted branches of a sick tree, like wounds that would never heal.

"Come on," Yvonne said. "Let's read. We don't have much time."

(From the writings of my father, done upon his return from camp in 1945.)

INMATE 130583 INTRODUCES HIMSELF:

I have many reasons to write this article for publication, but I would consider myself particularly lucky if it could appear in a neutral newspaper because I would like to tell you everything I went through in Germany's concentration camps during the last two years.

An enormous number of people were deported by the German barbarians, and only very few came back. Should somebody ask me today: "How come you are here?" Frankly, I would be at a loss to answer the question.

I live like in a dream and cannot grasp reality. I feel as though I have been projected sky high from the deepest abyss and actually do not know what is happening to me. Acquaintances and people I do not know approach me, offer me help, want to do something for me. I see them as through a haze and do not understand a thing!

Yes, indeed, I can compare myself to a newborn child for I have the same reactions! What has happened? Where am I? And where do I come from? Do miracles really happen in this world? Or is this the greatest miracle? Yes, I am alive. I, inmate 130583, and I am allowed to speak. I can tell about my suffering and scream so loudly that even the dead will hear me.

I assure you that I shall most carefully avoid dramatizing anything. I stand before you as before a world court:

I solemnly swear to tell the truth and nothing but the truth. I accuse the entire German nation and make it responsible before the whole world for the mass murders, for their cruel, crafty and ferocious lust to kill and destroy.

Oh yes! You "Kulturträger" (bearers of culture)! You "Weltbeglücker" (benefactors of the world)!, with your Goethe, Schiller, Kant, Nietzsche, Schopenhauer, with your Beethoven and Mozart.

I will create a symphony for you, which will project you into unspeak-

able horror and despair. Isn't it true that you have never been Nazis and that, of course, you never wanted to have this regime. And, of course, you had no idea what they were doing to us in the camps!.

Well! No harm done, you will hear it, you miserable nation with your double face, your double conscience, but no, you don't have a double heart — there is only a German heart, a heart of the worst murderers!

For you, poor, innocent women, for you, beloved, little Jewish children, for you, men, old and young, I will try to paint a picture. It is a gigantic task.

Where is the poet who will describe this suffering?

Where is the painter to paint these colors?

Sky about Birkenau. Sky about Auschwitz. The sun could hardly break through the dark blanket in the sky, the blanket which was smoke, heavy clouds of smoke; black clouds of smoke rising from the crematories where human beings were burned — these black clouds were always in the sky over Birkenau...

Birkenau, you were built in order to fry the entire Jewry in your crematories. The satanic spirit of the Nazi gangs produced a creation which fully corresponded to modern times.

German people! You really outdid yourself. If today there are still some Jews left, I can assure you that it means as many tragedies. Those are only shadows of human beings, who are lonely and alone, poor souls.

Well, now I will try to begin my story. Should you in the course of the narration encounter some gross expressions, please don't be shocked. They don't come from me, they belong to the "couleur locale" (local color).

Until my arrest we lived in Grenade-sur-Garonne, a little township near Toulouse. My family consisted of my mother, my wife, two small children and myself. Despite the hard times we led a quiet life. A happy little family.

On July 7, 1943, our fate was sealed. This was the day when my wife and I both died (I can say today that I was born twice: the first time March 7, 1902, the second time on April 11, 1945).

Well, on July 7, 1943, at seven in the morning, the Gestapo men came to our house. The two gentlemen introduced themselves as officials of the German economic police!

At home were my wife, my mother and myself. We had earlier already placed our children in a Catholic monastery.

So on this sad and memorable day we are asked to give information about the rich Jews in Grenade. We cannot and do not want to give such information. The gentlemen get impatient and tell us to pack a few things for a couple of days because our situation must also be clarified. When my old mother starts to weep, the representatives of the new order threaten to take her along, too.

The same night we are brought to the military prison. I am also separated from my wife. We remain 9 days in prison, without interrogation, and then, chained like the worst criminals, we are transported to Paris, that is to Drancy, where we are "liberated" from all our valuables, watches, rings, etc.

The next day, July 18, we are to join a transport to destination "U n - k n o w n ." We are told it is going to "Pitsche-Poi." We laughed about this expression because such a place did not exist. It was the spiritual product of the intellectual elite of Drancy.

We start at Bobigny. At the railroad station we are loaded into cattle cars — 70 persons with luggage in each car — men, women, children. The doors are locked, of course. Please don't forget it is the middle of the summer. We get a bucket and a pail of water. Even the most elementary needs must be relieved in the presence of the women, and vice versa.

At long last the train leaves, the journey lasts four days and four nights. Drancy and France are far away. Finally we arrive somewhere. But where are we?

The doors are thrown open. We try to find out where we are but all we see is a field on which we notice people in striped uniforms like prisoners at Sing-Sing, and all around we see SS men. By hitting us and pushing us with the butts of their rifles we are helped from the cattle cars.

"Leave the luggage here!" screams an SS man.

"Women, children, the old and the weak to the right!" is the next order.

Men are sent to the left. We obey the order without realizing that this is the beginning of the big "Adieu." I see my poor wife turning to the right. I have hardly time to say goodbye to her and I see her joining the crowd of women. I would never see her again.

We march forward and pass in front of high-ranking SS officers. Is it possible that these people have no scruples, no pity and treat us like a herd of cattle?

We are sorted out and are sent either to the right or to the left. I notice a number of trucks for those who cannot walk.

I also would like to get on a truck but the officer who looks me over decides otherwise. I am disappointed and join the group of those who must walk.

How could I know that for the time being I was to live! At this moment the lord and master over life and death pushes me to life.

All those who got on the trucks went to their deaths! They were immediately driven to the gas chamber, because we are in Birkenau or Auschwitz 2. I will draw you a little picture, give you a tiny description.

At Birkenau the German genius has shown what organization means, organization as thorough and grandiose as the world has ever seen. There were 4, or in letters four, crematories with adjoining gas chambers, where the useless Jew dirt filling the trucks was transformed into ashes within the shortest time. It was, so to say, a Chemical Enterprise.

Here are the names of these executioners who carried out the orders of their superiors.

1. The "Lagerführer" (camp commander) of "Birkenau." "Sturmführer"

2. The camp doctor of "Birkenau," Dr. Klein Schwartzhuber.

3. The camp "Rapportführer" "Oberscharführer" Schillinger.

4. The camp "Arbeitsdienstführer" "Oberscharführer" Graul.

They were all "Führer," rather small "Führer" but imitating the example of the great "Führer".

Only about twenty percent of those in our transport are taken to the camp; all the others are gassed, burned, and only the smoke that always lingers over Birkenau knows what happened to the rest.

We enter the camp. First we go to the "pre-camp," the so-called Sauna. There everything is taken from us. We are naked, all our hair is being shaved, then a number is tattooed on our left arm. My number is 130583. It was a good number, I must admit, because I returned, I came back. It was just like a lottery. Very few winners, but many, very many losers. This number is our "état civil." We are branded for life. I will keep it forever, and I am proud of it. And you, German "Kulturträger!" You are proud too, aren't you?

Our things are not returned to us. They are now the property of the German Reich. Instead dirty, stinking rags are thrown at us, no matter how they fit. We sink deeper and deeper. We can hardly remember how we looked an hour earlier. We are nothing but numbers. We get a bath without hardly any water and now we are the victims of German tyranny.

We remain the whole night — the fifth night — in this "pre-camp." We remain standing, almost naked, in an empty barrack, waiting for the coming day.

The next day we enter the main camp and are assigned to barrack 26. We are under the absolute rule of the "Blockälteste" (trustee) and his scribe. Those who want to find favor with the SS command must be devoid of any human feelings, and we are the most appropriate victims.

A "Blockälteste" held absolute power over life and death of inmates. If he disliked an inmate, he could send him without further ado to Jehovah. During my entire internment I have not seen a "Blockälteste" or his deputy without a club.

A prisoner who was to be liquidated was told:

"Bend down!" Several blows on the back of the neck, just as you kill a rabbit. The next day his card was sent to the office with the remark: died. And that was all!

The SS were not interested to know why somebody had died. After all, there were so many Jews and sooner or later it would be everybody's turn.

We are brought to the barrack and our new master receives us with a welcoming speech. He says as follows:

"You dirty scum, you are here in Birkenau. You will learn right away what that means. No one leaves from here. There is one way out — through the chimney. Here you must work till you croak. Those who don't want to work or expect something else, can get it over with very quickly. Here at the barbed wire. It is electrified."

We are standing there and are beginning to realize what is happening. I am thinking of my poor wife, what has happened to her and where is she now?

In the barrack we see two rows of bunks, wooden bunks. With blows we are driven to the bunks, ten men to a bunk which is meant for five.

We notice a number of educational inscriptions:

Take your caps off in the barrack.

Keep clean, because cleanliness is your health.

A louse, your death.

Don't steal from your comrade,

because you steal his life.

Be disciplined, freedom through work.

So that is our new domicile and the sixth night without sleep. We are given coats of former Russian prisoners of war and we try to sleep. But it is impossible, we are attacked by lice, armies of lice. We are horrified. We think of the warning inscription and begin to laugh. A louse, your death.

We are awakened at 4:30 a.m. We are getting up at top speed, with the help of blows falling all over us. We are supposed to wash ourselves in the washrooms, but at present there are only two washrooms for 120 inmates in our sector. Our turn never comes because the old veterans come first and there is hardly any water at all. We are again reminded of the inscription: keep clean. But how can we wash ourselves without water? Towels, of course, are an unknown quantity, not to speak of soap. For over three months I used my cap as a towel.

But, we have to be clean because the "Blockälteste" is wielding his club and the blows are falling. We curse the day we were born and start thinking of the electrified barbed wire.

We spend the first day in front of our barrack and find out about our food rations.

We are supposed to receive — I say supposed to because we never receive it all — in the morning some slop smelling like German coffee, at noon 3/4 of a litre of soup, at night one bread for four, with a trace of margarine or a thin slice of sausage. This is the official ration of the SS administration which is a starvation ration anyway, but the "Blockälteste" and his general staff are prisoners, too, receiving the same ration, and they need, of course, much more than the ordinary ration, so what else can they do but steal?

Pieces are cut off the bread as well as from any other food we are getting, and the poor, helpless inmate gets even less. As I said, any means are good enough to make life an unbearable burden.

The same day we are assigned to work teams. I am assigned to a barracks-building team. If a trustee is the ruler in the barracks, so the teams are ruled by the "Kapos." Oh, these dear "Kapos"! These gentlemen are selected from among the worst criminals, and do they love us.

My "Kapo," a fellow condemned to life in prison, leads us the next morning to our work place. We are to unload the whole day's building material. The work is made even more difficult because of the blows raining down on us. We collapse under the load and the blows but are somehow getting up again. The "Kapo" can just as easily launch us into eternity as the "Blockälteste." At night we are marched back to the camp and at the entrance an orchestra plays German marches (please, don't laugh!). I remain with this team for three weeks and I am at the end of my strength.

I manage to get into another team called "Weichseldurchstich" (Weichsel-piercing). The work place is about 6 km. from the camp and on the way we are guarded by SS men with dogs. While we march the SS guards are setting the dogs against us, just for fun. Some of us arrive seriously bitten at our work place.

We are standing at a canal which must be regulated. For this purpose we must undress completely. The leader of the team, an SS "Hauptscharführer," tells the "Kapos" that it is forbidden to beat the prisoners — we do not believe our ears but soon we understand, because he adds: "at least not to death."

We crawl into the mud. The SS men watch from both banks shouting: "Work, you stinking Jews!" We shovel without stopping, because our watchers are watching! Suddenly I am called.

The "Kapo" and the leader of the team stand in front of me.

"Dirty Jew, why don't you work??"

I take the liberty of saying I do work.

But that is as far as it goes.

"Bend down" is the command.

I am naked and I must obey the order. I am flogged on my behind with a rubber-hose — ten blows. I return to my work. Several prisoners are called. They are supposed to fetch something beyond the line of guards. The poor devils want to please and start running. But they don't run far, we hear shots.

When we return to the camp, the "Kapo" reports:

"Team "Weichseldurschstick," 300 prisoners, number correct, 9 prisoners shot while trying to escape." We carry nine corpses and the orchestra plays marches to make our marching look smart.

The next day we experience the first "selection."

This word should forever be stricken from the dictionary. What is a "selection"?

We are forbidden to leave the barrack, we undress completely. Then an SS doctor appears and looks us over, every one. If he thinks a man is skinny, weak, unable to work, he notes his number.

This happens in all the barracks, and there are quite a lot whose numbers *are taken. The next day those marked for death are taken to special barracks to be gassed, according to program. The Birkenau chimneys are always working to capacity.*

Nearby is the camp for women, and conditions there are even worse. An enormous number of women are selected for death in the gas chambers. One day we are returning from work and on the road encounter cars loaded with naked women on their way to the gas chambers. They scream at us:

"Revenge! Take revenge!"

But we can only stare because we are still holding on to our miserable life.

I manage again to get out of my team and am assigned to the team "Klarenanlage" (sewerage plant). There we must carry bricks and cement all day long. I collapse. I am being beaten so much that I am getting used to it. After all it is a matter of habit.

By an improbable series of circumstances I manage to get into a team which actually saves my life. I am assigned to an administrative team as a clerk. Nobody is beaten there. I do my work so efficiently that my boss, an SS Führer pulls me out of a transport of prisoners who are sent to Warsaw for cleaning-up work. (Only a few returned to Birkenau where they were gassed.) I learn that my wife is alive, that she is in Auschwitz in Barrack 10.

What can I tell you about that barrack? Maybe you should ask the camp commander, "Sturmführer" Hessler about it? Four-hundred-fifty to five hundred Jewish women lived in barrack 10. They were used as guinea pigs for experiments with artificial insemination. They also carried out other experiments such as removing internal organs from 16 - 17 year old girls and then throwing the girls into the oven as useless rubbish.

Now I know that my wife is alive and lives in that barrack. I manage to correspond with her once which, of course, is done very secretly and is extremely dangerous. My wife writes me: "You don't know where I am. What does it matter if I get one more or one less injection if I could only hope to see you again in this life!"

Perhaps! Perhaps! Perhaps some day we will get out of this hell. The hope is very slim but we don't want to give up. We are hoping for a miracle which may, after all, happen one day. The "selections" continue, new transports arrive and the crematories are working full speed.

On March 1, 1944 I am moved to another camp. I am sent to Monowitz, also called Buna. Monowitz is situated along the highway between Kattowitz and Cracow, about 55 km. from the latter town. There I.G. Farben has built several factories which are steeped in our blood. Jewish hands have been toiling there and you, Dr. Duerrfeld, director general of I.G. Auschwitz, will confirm it!

The camp is ruled by the camp "Führer" (Lagerführer) "Hauptsturmführer" Schettel.

The "Lagerkommandant" "Hauptsturmführer" Schwarz,

The "Kommandoführer" "Hauptscharführer" Rakers,

The "Arbeitsdienstführer" — "Hauptscharführer" Stolten.

One thing does not exist here — no gas chambers. But there are other means — hanging.

Each Sunday we are forced to attend the same spectacle. We gather at the assembly place in order to witness the ceremony. The verdict is read to the condemned:

"SS Reichsführer" Himmler etc." and then follows the hanging. Later we have to pass in front of the corpses in order to see what a hanged man looks like. The accusation? Attempt to flee, sabotage, just anything.

We get so used to it that it seems strange if a Sunday goes by without the hanging procedure. After the hanging there is the football match. After that the orchestra plays and in the evening we have to march past a special barrack. In order to watch, how the Aryan inmates enter the barrack to amuse themselves for 20 minutes with a lady assigned to them.

This is, of course, strictly forbidden to Jews and is punished by execution. The barrack in which 12-15 Aryan women live is fenced in and the "entertainment" starts when a bell rings and stops when the bell rings again.

We work very hard in Buna, together with numerous German civilians and English prisoners of war. Only our striped prison garb distinguishes us from them.

I am acting as an interpreter, because there are many Poles, Russians and Frenchmen. The plant keeps growing and growing until one day we receive a visit. A visit from above. "All good things come from above" says a German proverb and, indeed, one day the Americans show up from above.

What has been painstakingly built in the course of years is turned into ashes in a quarter of an hour, but the plant is so huge that several visits are required.

They are coming again and again until the whole thing is smashed to smithereens. We are put to work to clean up the place but we are in no hurry. We have plenty of time and the SS slowly begin to understand the situation. Is it because the Russians are at Lemberg???

However, life continues, so does the hanging, but one Sunday we get some satisfaction. Three Jews are being hanged. As always we are standing there, listening to the reading of the verdict.

However, suddenly we hear another voice crying out:

"Comrades, brothers, don't despair, we are the last to be hanged, after us this scum will hang. Courage, the day must come when these murderers will hand on the gallows."

Trembling with rage, the "Lagerführer" screams furiously: "Faster, faster, hurry up."

And all we hear from the gallows is a quotation from Götz von Berlichingen. The poor victims were not entirely right but neither were they entirely wrong.

I remain at the Buna camp until September 17, 1944. Then I am sent to Gleiwitz 2.

In Gleiwitz there were only four camps at that time and I am assigned to Gleiwitz 2 which is a small camp holding about 700 men and 300 *women (who are in a separate camp). At this camp there were installations for the production of soot which in turn was used for the production of artificial rubber. In Germany everything was artificial.*

Only one thing was real — the blows that were raining down on us. Every evening after roll call a few poor guys are selected and the "Lagerführer" "Oberscharführer" Dietrichsen whips their behinds to shreds. The reason? One has swiped a turnip, another has gorged on potato peels, a third one forgot to take off his cap when meeting an SS man.

The victims are obliged to count the blows aloud, and since there are mainly Polish Jews whose German is not very good, they may be saying "Nein" instead of "Neun" and they are whipped cruelly until they pronounce the word properly.

Sometimes it happens that a prisoner manages to escape. As punishment all the inmates of the camp have to remain standing on the assembly place. We were once standing at attention for ten hours. It was winter, many could hardly stand but the SS watched and if someone as much as wobbled, a shot from a pistol finished him off. The next morning there were corpses in front of each barrack.

There was also a medical barrack, but woe to those who fell sick. Who needs parasites? I saw prisoners who had typhus reporting for work, for they knew that to be sick mean to be dead. I saw inmates walking around with phlegmon. Their wounds so gaping that my fist would fit in. They were crawling with millions of maggots but they did not report to the medical barrack.

We had a "Blockführer" who had a special idea of a joke. Once he had the whole barrack awakened at 1 a.m. We had to jump down from our bunks at full speed, undress completely and then he chased us around outside the barracks under a pouring rain. Because we were so dirty we should take a bath, but first go through some physical exercises.

"Fall down, get up, fall down, get up, roll on the ground, jump, roll on the ground, run."

We could hardly breathe, we were covered with dirt from head to toe. Then we were ordered to take our bath, that is, to stand under the pouring rain. We were cursing God in heaven. After two hours we were permitted to return to the barrack. He was standing at the door with a whip, whipping our poor, wet, naked bodies. Then he declared:

"Now you will all get pneumonia and you will go all the way up."

A prisoner is caught, trying to escape. He is brought before the "Rapportführer" Schilliger and the following dialogue ensues:

"Why did you want to scram, dirty Jew?"

"Because I wanted to live." is the answer.

"Don't you know that a Jew has no right to live?"

"Yes, Herr Rapportführer."

"Do you know anything about astronomy?"

"No, Herr Rapportführer."

"Where is the Milky way?"

"I don't know."

"Look up into the sky, that's where you are going."

A shot in the neck dispatches him to the Milky Way.

The last action against the Jews took place in Hungary. An enormous number of Jews were brought to the camp and the four crematories could hardly manage their work.

They had to find another solution. After being gassed, the victims were burned on stakes.

The citizens of the city of Auschwitz complained in Berlin. They could stand the stench of burnt flesh no longer.

Jews were brought from Crete by submarines. We were indeed a precious commodity.

Everyone wonders whether these beasts will ever have to pay. Is there a commensurate punishment for these murderers, these criminals?

No! It is impossible, what shall we do, what can we do?

There is only one thing — we must never forget!

If I am today reunited with my children, the threatening specter of the innumerable victims rises ominously before my eyes, calling. Do not forget!

On my way back home I saw that Germany today was nothing but rubble and ashes. The once so proud cities were lying in ruins. I was reminded of Hitler's promise: "Give me ten years' time and you will not recognize Germany!"

(Original writings in Photo/Document section)

The second candle was almost burnt out, its white creamy residue flattened out all around the saucer.

"We must return the notebook before Papa gets up," Yvonne said. I looked up. Her eyes were swollen, all red. I could hardly see through mine.

"Be careful down the ladder," she said, as she held out her hand to help me down.

18

NANITA

N anita had come the first Saturday morning after our return to Grenade.

"Let's go to the fields," she said. "We'll pick berries and make ice cream."

She looked the same as long ago, that day we had said goodbye after the truck, left taking Papa and Maman away. Not very tall, a bit on the plump side. Not slim and svelte like Maman. Her pale narrow face resembled a madonna's. I was often reminded of it as I prayed to the statues of Sainte-Marie in the convent. Everything was so perfect. The oval dark brown eyes, the narrow nose, the rounded full lips, the short brown hair, carefully groomed.

Her hands held a special fascination for me. They were soft and slim with perfect nails, long and crimson colored. Two fingers on her left hand were slightly bent, giving it a graceful allure. I used to admire and caress it. She always laughed, showing me how she could not flatten the fingers out due to rheumatism and was unable to understand why I liked the way her infirmity looked.

We had met in Grenade. Many people had run away from Paris at the beginning of the war, trying to find a corner where they would be safe. The river La Garonne was so beautiful. Before Yvonne and I went to the convent, Maman used to take me there every day to bathe and play in the sand along its banks. I carried a little pail and shovel and followed Maman, sometimes tripping on my little open sandals.

Maman often talked to people who also came there but, mostly, she liked to find a private corner so she could practice her singing, which she loved to do for hours and hours.

I saw the beautiful lady looking at us as we walked on the country dirt road bordered by wild flowers and thorny black-berry bushes. I looked down to the ground afraid to meet her gaze. She came closer and started talking to Maman introducing herself. *"Bonjour Madame,"* she said, "my name is Madeleine. May I share the walk. I presume you are heading for the river?"

"Yes, of course." Maman replied. "My name is Annette, and this is my younger daughter Renée."

The pretty lady bent down, and looked deep into my eyes. *"Bonjour!* What a beautiful child!" she exclaimed.

We walked on and she chatted with Maman, explaining how she had landed in this village. She kept looking toward me and then she said: "Would you like to come home with me and be my little girl? I do not have the good fortune to have a child and would so love to have you."

I grabbed Maman's hand and squeezed it tightly. *"Non, Madame, merci.* I already have a mother, and I want to stay with her," I whispered.

Being so young, I had taken her seriously. The fairy tale books were full of stories of children being stolen, dragged to far away places where mysterious happenings occurred.

I quickly changed sides and grabbed Maman's other hand so I would not be near her. They both started to laugh. "Don't worry," Maman said "You are my treasure. I will never give you away."

As time went on the lady gradually befriended Maman and came with us all the time. Slowly, I gained confidence and let her brush my long black hair and tell me enchanting stories. She met us almost every day, and I knew it was mostly for me that she came.

She lovingly told me how much she always had wanted a child like me, and that her greatest misfortune in life was not being a mother. By now I knew she would not steal me, so I let her indulge her maternal tenderness, making believe I was a little bit her child during those sunny afternoons.

Maman told me I could call her *tante* (aunt) Madeleine, but that was long and formal and she said no, she didn't like being called that. She really would have wanted me to call her Maman, but that was out of the question.

"Why don't you call me Nanita?" she suggested, explaining it was an endearing term used in Spain by children to call their nannies. She had lived there for many years. So we decided that was a good name, and all called her Nanita from that day on.

She lived in a small house the other end of town. You had to pass the large cathedral, the main square and lots of little streets to get there.

She shared her home with Parrain. He was a large man with a big bush of red hair. He came from the north, an English-speaking country, but he had lived in France all his life so you really couldn't tell. Sometimes Parrain would teach us English words.

We had such fun trying to imitate him as he used to say: "Think h-h-o-t-t, like if you have a boiling potato in your mouth. Then it will come out all right!"

Parrain knew Nanita in Paris. When he left, his big car loaded with as much as he could take, he had persuaded her there was much danger in the north and she should come along with him to the south. I heard Papa and Maman say many times: "When will she finally agree? Francis keeps saying they should get married — what is she waiting for?"

I wasn't quite sure what the fuss was about. One day, I had heard Papa and Maman discuss what had happened to her. She had been unhappily married and divorced at a young age. Then she had gone to live in Spain with a count, or a duke, whom she loved so much. He had been forced to marry a noble Spanish woman chosen for him and Nanita had to return to France.

I heard Papa and Maman talk about her, saying how she told them that when she left her castle, twelve guards would throw their capes on the ground for her to walk on lest she should soil the soles of her shoes on her way to mount the waiting carriage.

It sounded so grand, like the tales in the picture books I stared at for hours. I made believe it was her face in the stories, dressed in long silky gowns, wearing a crown.

Time passed. Love became easier between us. I heard Maman once ask Nanita if she would look after Yvonne and me should anything happen to Papa and her. I didn't understand why Maman said such things. It frightened me.

Then, that day, when the truck took Papa and Maman away, and we were saying goodbye to her and Parrain before returning to the convent, she said: "I have always wanted you to be my child. But not this way! Not this way!" she had repeated sadly, as she helped pack the little bag I was taking back to the convent.

Now I looked at her, one hand on the handle bar holding the bicycle, the other gesturing me to the back seat. Perhaps somewhere, long ago in another world, it had been written that I would belong to her after all and be the child she never had and craved for.

She took me in back of her bicycle. I knew she wanted to talk, be alone with me, get reacquainted, go back to the past. She seemed to search for words before speaking. I could tell she wasn't sure. "Let's sit for a minute on this bench, under the shade of that tree," she said.

I suddenly felt the same resentment as that first day we met, and I had held on to Maman's hand, worried she might steal me from her. I wasn't going to let her be my mother. I wasn't going to let anyone be my mother. Of this I was certain.

"We'll be leaving to return to Paris soon," she said. "Do you think you might want to come to live with us? I am planning to speak to your father about it."

"No Nanita," I said, without hesitation. "I will stay with Oma, Papa and Yvonne, no matter what."

"But your Oma is very old. Your Papa is not well, and not as he was before. Your sister's almost sixteen. She is very grown up. I don't think she'll be around for long. I would like to adopt you. Parrain and I love you as our child. We are man and wife now. You'll be happy with us."

A rage took over me. I jumped up from the bench. Why! Oh why! did this happen to us? We were nothing. Just broken pieces that could never be mended. "No. Never. You hear. Never. Do not ask me again. I belong to them. Only to them, and to Maman," I shouted.

I ran home so fast my feet were bloody from hitting stones on the narrow earth road. I banged the wooden door with my fists and almost made Oma fall as I ran into her, throwing my arms around her waist, clutching the ever present apron.

"Oma, you'll keep me? Won't you? I'll take care of myself. I won't ask much. Don't let Papa give me away. I must stay with you. Always. Promise, Oma, promise." I insisted, as Oma dried my tears with the corner of the apron and caressed my head reassuringly.

Am I this child?
Without warmth.
Without love.

This child
who must learn
laws of life
in cold streams?
Fighting thorns that prickle.
needles that bite.

Am I this child?
Without a mother.
The comfort of her wings
to shelter me.

19

NOW
WE
KNOW
FOR
SURE

O ne day a woman came to our door.

"I am Lela," she said. "May I come in? You must be Maurice's mother. I have some news for him."

Oma called Papa and he came running to the door. We came up from the back room when we heard the commotion.

Papa embraced Lela. I remembered she was the woman Papa had given a ride to when he was liberated — she had come from a nearby camp.

"Have you found your husband, your children, your parents?" Papa exclaimed anxiously.

Lela shook her head and tears filled her eyes. "No. No one," she said. "No one is left."

"Come in. Come in. You can stay here as long as you like," Papa said, taking Lela by the hand into the front room, asking Oma to set one more plate on the table where we were to have lunch.

"Do you know what happened to them?" Papa asked.

"No. Not yet. The authorities are trying to get some details. It will take time," Lela answered. "I came because I met some women who had been with your wife. I thought you would like to hear what happened to her."

Papa's face got hard and his lips started to quiver. "Yes. I want to know. Please tell me," he said looking at her sharply.

"Not yet," Lela answered, looking in our direction. "I am tired from the journey. May we first eat, and then we'll talk. I would like to be alone with you then. Is that all right?"

"Yes," Papa said. He understood. Lela didn't want us there. Lela didn't want us to hear what happened to Maman.

After the meal they left. Many hours later, when they finally returned, Papa went into the room and told Oma he would like to be alone. He looked ill. Drained.

"What is he going to do?" I asked Yvonne with a worried look.

"I saw him take out the notebook and the pen. I think he is

going to write. I don't think he can talk about it."

We saw the faint candlelight through the bottom of the door as darkness approached. Papa did not leave the room the whole next day. At night Yvonne told me we would wait for him to sleep and take the notebook to the barn as we had done the last time. When we finally did, we stared at the first page and we saw Papa had written in large letters.

"MY WIFE IS NO LONGER HERE.
I SHALL TESTIFY ON HER BEHALF.
THIS IS WHAT I FEEL SHE WOULD SAY IF SHE WERE ALIVE."

"These happenings were related to me from information of other inmates who shared the pains with her, but had the good fortune to survive."

(From the writings of my father, done upon his return from camp in 1945, after his liberation)

I would like to start my report by telling you about Barrack 10 in Auschwitz. But I really don't know whether I am able to do it, because it is almost beyond human strength to put it all down on paper. I will start with my first impressions:

Auschwitz was a camp for men with about 27,000 inmates at that time.

Barrack 10 was an isolated barrack only for women. The women were held there for a special purpose. Upon arrival the woman are led into a shower room where they have to undress in the presence of the SS and other male inmates.

Many resist but they are beaten and eventually everyone stands there naked. Their heads are shaven and the hair is removed from the whole body — all this in the presence of the SS. There are women of various nationalities in the barrack and the newly arrived learn what they have to expect. There is talk of big and small operations, of all kinds of injections, but above all of gas, because this barrack is supposedly the medical barrack, and sick people are speedily "dispatched."

The danger of getting sick is so great that most of the women are resigned to their fate. They all know that, once here, you are doomed to die. Sooner, or later, who cares.

My wife is assigned to Professor Glauber as a guinea pig for experiments.

I am asking myself:

What has been going on in the minds of these murderers? Could normal people do such things? Or were we in the hands of a gang of notorious criminals and sadists?

These scoundrels, with their professor or doctor titles, wanted to work on artificial insemination with Jewish women. They wanted to give a present to the world, at the expense of our women. The world had already received a number of German blessings, but this would be the crowning glory of German science!

Three days after her arrival at barrack 10, my wife, or rather the number of my wife (the women are also tattooed like the men and her number was 50352) is called. She is brought into an operating room, where she experiences her first tortures. She is given an enormous injection into her inner organs causing excruciating pain. She is carried back to her barrack because she cannot walk. She remains paralyzed for 48 hours and feels as though she would burst. These treatments are repeated regularly every four weeks but, in between, the Jewish women must work very hard. They must carry bricks, build roads, transport sand or gravel and are beaten just like the men.

This happens in the twentieth century. It is planned and carried out consciously and with blind hatred by men who have sworn to exterminate us by all means.

We don't know anything about each other. We don't know the fate of our children because we are never allowed to write. We are, in the literal sense of the word, buried alive.

My wife remained for over 18 months in barrack 10.

Many women during that time went the way to Birkenau.

The barracks are steadily supplied with fresh material for there were still many Jews left and they were brought from all the countries grabbed by Hitler. Jews are brought from Greece, even from Crete they are brought in submarine. We are a precious commodity for these gentlemen.

Is it an unshakable faith? Is it a pure accident that my wife endures it all up to that point. She has become hardened in the course of time and knows how to beat the system. In other words, she has become an "old timer" and enjoys a certain respect.

Poor, suffering human beings, most of them did not survive the first weeks.

But life continues and everyone clings to the childish hope. Perhaps, perhaps! From their barrack the women can see the nearby "Beskiden." There is freedom, free people live there. Free, happy people, but here is the cold reality, the electrified barbed wire. Here, we are in the hands of the SS gangsters.

On January 17, 1945 the camp at Auschwitz is also evacuated. Only barrack 10 remains. An order is received to gas the whole barrack. There should be no witnesses, but it is too late. At Birkenau the inmates have blown up two crematories and the Russians are close.

Now Papa continued as though he was speaking through Maman's voice, as though he knew what she would say.

Oh! they were deadly afraid of the Russians, these heroes. My God! They ran faster than the Russians. All those men have left a few hours ago and we still do not know what will happen to us.

Late at night we are assembled and march into the unknown. We are on the road for three days and three nights until we reach Glogau. There we are loaded into open cattle cars and travel for a whole week without any food. We lick the snow and beg the SS to give us some snow from the ballast. They do it, but they mix the snow with coal dust. At last we arrived at Ravensbruck.

At the Ravensbruck camp there was feverish activity, for transports kept arriving from the whole Reich. It was the beginning of the end.

We are ordered into a tent, into which about 3000 persons are squeezed. We lack everything. We cannot wash and we get no food for a long time.

As a result of swallowing snow I get a severe stomach and intestinal infection. I become a Muslim (the name given to those who were candidates for the crematory). I am running a high fever and am taken to the "Revier" (sick room) where I remain for four weeks.

There I meet a Polish woman doctor to whom I owe my life, because one day we hear a "selection" is due.

We know what that means because here, too, they have gas. The Polish doctor explains the danger to me.

I want to live. I want to live so badly. I am so young. I want to see my children again, my husband. With a superhuman effort I pull myself together and ask immediately to be reported as fit for work.

I am assigned to a barrack and must work. I am trying to do as little as possible as long as possible but one day I am caught and brought before the "Arbeitsdienstführer." The scoundrel screams at me: "You dirty Jew female, you don't want to work, you shirk work. I will teach you to work."

Suddenly, he is hitting me in the face with his fists until I am black and blue. I fall down and while lying on the ground I get kicked in the behind.

As punishment I am assigned to the forest team. There we must fell trees, drag heavy trunks to the road, and load them on trucks. If someone collapses, the bastards get her back on her feet in a hurry. I could not endure this regime for too long.

With the greatest difficulties I manage to get assigned to the potato team. There things are better because while we load potatoes we manage occasionally to hide a few rotten potatoes which we eat raw.

However, other events are shaping up which greatly excite us. We hear of tremendous breakthroughs at all fronts. The United Nations are deep in Germany and we begin to indulge in politics and strategy. We see the collapse coming. We feel the approach of extraordinary events.

Then, Papa stopped talking as though he was Maman, and he wrote: *"No one knows what happened to her after that. No one knows what her end was. And I, shall forever wonder how it came..."*

Yvonne reached out, taking my hands. We couldn't speak. Our throats were locked. "Well, now we know. Now we know for sure," she finally said.

As she closed the notebook, a yellowed paper, wrinkled and dirty-looking fell out from the back. It was Papa's handwriting. The ink was black and it looked very old.

(Original writings in Photo/Document section)

This poem was written in the camp of Birkenau and dedicated to my beloved wife, who was only three kilometers away from me, but whom I never could see.

IT'S ANNETTE'S BIRTHDAY

My friends asked me this morning
What all this meant.
They wanted to know my trouble,
They wanted to know who was Annette.

All through the night, they said.
Her name was murmured by you.
Is this woman so dear to you
And where does she stay right now?

They bothered me to no end with stupid questions.
And kept pestering me, the fools.

In the end, I was forced to tell them
That today Annette was born.

Annette, I said.
Is the blood of my heart.
She is not far from here
And suffers as much as I do.

Not so long ago, it's hardly a year,
We thought life was beautiful.
We were all gathered in a room
And everyone offered his best.

We showered her with presents.
We were gay and joyous.
We danced, we laughed,
And Renée recited a poem.
The poem about a rose, her young life
And little Renée wishing
To give it to her Mamy
Without crying.

Who could foresee that hardly a year later
Fate caught up with us, too.
And that we could not spent this beautiful day
Together with our beloved ones.

I told you all that
To satisfy your curiosity.
You have bothered me enough
And now just leave me alone, I pray.

They went away, I was alone
And I felt so miserably sad
Thinking of my lost happiness,

Thinking of my poor darling wife.

I climbed up to my shabby bunk,
My world was dark and sad,
Patiently I waited for Annette to come
But she could not come, my darling.

Outside the day was slowly breaking,
I did not want to wait for the gong.
A new day is dawning with the same grief and trouble,
With the same backbreaking work.

Lela left the next day.

20

THE
MESSAGE

Yvonne went back to the big school where you had one class for all the subjects, but you had other teachers for cooking and sewing.

Her teacher, Mademoiselle Pradère was tall and skinny with dark hair tied in a chignon way up on top. The color was a mix of black and gray. She wore long dark skirts and blouses buttoned all the way to the edge of her neck. Her shoes were flat with laces carefully tied. She was very strict.

I wished I could be in the same school with Yvonne but for my age there was a separate building, and we had only one teacher for everything.

The first few days I didn't speak to anyone. As soon as the bell rang in the courtyard I would run out and wait for Yvonne further up the street where her school was, and we would walk home together.

In the courtyard at recess everyone jumps rope, runs in games of hide and seek, or plays ball. I stand in the corner, looking. They don't care, I think. They go home and everything is the same. Their world hasn't stopped breathing like mine did. They don't cry to go to sleep, like I do.

They don't climb out the window Sunday morning to go to early Mass, hiding from their Oma. They go out the front door, all dressed up for Sunday eleven o'clock Mass, the whole family proudly walking to the church. Then, they go home for a big meal, and their Maman is there, and mine is gone, and I will never see her again.

Who am I anyway? My Oma lights Sabbath candles, prays under her lace shawl, and tells me stories from the bible, saying:

"Don't forget who you are."

But I don't know. I don't know anymore... Why must I pray to one God, but belong to another?

The teacher comes and takes my hand. "Come on, Renée. You must participate. Recess is for stretching, running, and getting some exercise. Your mind works better after that. Come, join the others," she insists.

Slowly I become acquainted with some of the children.

"Where were you before here?" they ask. They don't know anyone who hasn't been here all their lives.

One girl becomes a little bit my friend. But I am careful. If you get to like someone, usually something happens. They disappear, or you must leave, and then you lose the person's friendship, and you are alone again.

She lives a little higher up on our street. We walk together. Yvonne is happy I don't follow her everywhere. She likes to be with the older girls.

My friend's name is Janine. She asks a lot of questions, and I tell her some things.

Then, one day, we were throwing a ball to each other in the school yard. I loved it there. The big trees shield you like giant umbrellas. The dirt floor feels soft under foot. There are inviting benches, where you can rest just before the small bell is pulled on top of the classroom door, telling you recess is over and calling you to go in.

Janine reached into her pocket to pick up something and threw it. As I caught it, it hit the palm of my hand with force and I realized it was not the bouncy ball we usually returned to each other back and forth.

Janine had thrown me an apple. She started laughing at my surprise. She pulled another out and ran over to me while biting into it.

"Hey, come on," she said. "Eat it before the bell."

"No. I can't. I am not going to eat this one."

"What do you mean? I really don't understand what you do sometimes," she added, looking a little annoyed.

"I had a friend once, and..." I couldn't finish the sentence.

"Well, you had a friend once, and..." she repeated, mimicking me.

I knew Janine wasn't going to stop until I told her. If I didn't, maybe she would tell everyone I was strange.

"You won't repeat?" I asked.

"No. No, of course." She was anxious now. I could see her curiosity growing. "We have another ten minutes. Come here and tell me," she said, dragging me to a corner bench that was deserted.

"Look," I said," it was long ago. It happened in the convent."

It was hard to talk about. I had never told anyone. Not even Yvonne. It seemed so far away, but I knew it was special. Something I would never forget.

"It was a message. You understand?"

Janine shook her head. "No. I don't. Why don't you explain?" she insisted.

I looked up to the sky, closed my eyes, and told her, trying to feel once more the magic of that moment.

It was so strong
I think of it as lightning.
But lightning,
in the middle of the day.
With the sun
brightly shining in your eyes!

The "message"
came to me through an apple!
I shall never forget this day!
It was on a Sunday.
It was late summer.
Almost fall.

The sun was shining so bright! It seemed to smile at me, as though something special was going to happen.

We jumped rope, ran around the yard, and then heard the bell summon us.

Sisters Marie-Paule, and Marie-Jeanne carried a huge basket

of red apples and deposited their charge while we gathered around.

Joy of joys!

First apples of the season!

We were each to get one.

A very rare treat!

My apple was red, a little touch of green on the side. The skinny stem curved gently, just long enough to hold, so you could admire this treasure from all sides.

I started walking.

No. I couldn't hurt such a pretty thing, and merely swallow it.

Lovely apple.

First, I will polish you,

shine you, smell you, admire you.

The apple became shiny like a mirror in whose reflection I could see my face. I held it up to the light and it became a star, throwing its blinding rays out to the universe! And then, I breathed its scent. And the apple told me the earth was moist, and warm and I should not despair.

"I am your friend," the apple said, "and my goal is to give you a message and a special wish! So now, decide what I can do for you and your wish will come true!"

"My wish is that you find Papa, and Maman, and Oma, and that we be together again.

My wish is for them to come and take me back.

My wish is to be just me, once more.

My wish is that I never forget,

what you taught me today.

That the sun shone on me.

That you were red and green.

That you glittered,

and smelled sweet.

That life will always be beautiful,

somehow, somewhere,

that hope should never be lost."

I sobbed, as I took my first bite, and the juice ran down my neck.

Janine looked at me, eyes wide open. "Did this really happen to you? You're sure you didn't dream it up?"

"I am sure," I said.

"Well, then. You think this apple is the same?"

"No. No apple will ever be the same," I answered her with sadness.

Just in case, I wasn't taking a chance, I thought, as I tucked the apple in my school apron pocket.

I got up to join the line in front of the classroom door, as *Mademoiselle* Colette was pulling the long cord, the bell calling us to go in.

21

THE
CANDY
MAN

The letter came in a large blue envelope. It was addressed to both Papa and Maman in round curly letters that looked like flowers.

"Who is it from?" we asked, as the mailman handed the letter to Oma.

"It's from Paris," she said. "I think it's from my niece Fanny." Oma turned the letter over to see who the sender's name was.

"I won't open it. It's for your parents. I mean your Papa," she quickly corrected herself looking at us sadly.

Papa meant everything to Oma. She'd have given her life for him. But still, one day, she had said to us: "Children need a mother. If one of them had to survive, it should have been her."

Oma had lost so much in her life. I had never met my Opa, Papa's father. He had died before I was born. In a sanatorium in Switzerland, of tuberculosis, I had heard, not really knowing what the word meant. He went to stay in the mountains, because the fresh air was supposed to cure him, but it never did.

We had heard many tales about him. How he was the head of a fine private school for boys. How he enjoyed music, opera, the arts, and had given the same loves to his son Maurice, my Papa.

There was also much talk of Alexander, Papa's younger brother. He also got tuberculosis and went to the same sanatorium. Alexander died shortly after his father. He wasn't twenty yet. Oma had her picture taken standing next to his grave, holding on to the stone. They said her hair turned silver overnight.

Oma came to live with us soon after Papa married Maman. I never remembered the house without her. I loved Oma almost as much as Papa and Maman. When they left in the morning in the big car to go to work, it was Oma who was home and picked me up at nursery school.

It is with her that I baked the little rolls, and made the dough for the noodles she prepared every Friday for the chicken soup. She let me stand next to her on a little stool so I could see. We'd arrange the flour and the eggs and the water, first making a little white mountain with a hole in the center in which we carefully poured the liquid things. We slowly moved the flour over to the middle and started to mix everything together. Our hands were sticky and the dough clung to our fingers like big bulky gloves.

"Mix. Mix hard," Oma would say. "Here, add some flour." And she would sprinkle the white snow on my hands to dry them a bit. Then she gathered the whole thing together and pushed down hard with the palm of her right hand, turning the ball around and around until it grew under her expert fingers and became shiny and bouncy. Then, the large wooden roller would come out. She pounded and stretched in all directions. For this operation I was a spectator only. Once the dough was smooth, the large pointy knife sliced through, making equal strips which she piled one on top of the other.

"Now your turn!" Oma would say, as she handed the small knife to me. My tongue stuck out as I carefully applied pressure and sliced down as evenly as I could.

Oma placed the little noodles on a tray, sprinkling them with flour and stacking them into a mountain.

"Come and do this now," she'd say, after a little while, as we switched positions around the table. Clap, clap, clap on the wood board, and the noodles jumped quickly from her expert hands as if they were a machine.

I looked at Oma now. She didn't look as big and strong as she had in those days. "Oma, where was aunt Fanny all these years?" I asked.

She was Papa's first cousin, the daughter of one of Oma's sisters. I faintly remembered her black eyes and slender face, that almost looked like a twin to Papa.

"I don't know, I hope they all hid and are fine. I hope my sister is alive," Oma said, with a worried look, clutching the letter, rubbing the envelope between her hands.

When Papa came home, she gave him the letter. She looked at his face, as his eyes moved from left to right, following the flowered lines down the page and then on the reverse side. Papa read slowly. He looked sad. When he finished, he handed the letter to Oma. Her hand was trembling. "Will I see them again?" she asked.

Papa did not reply. He just shook his head left to right in a gesture that meant no. Oma didn't read the letter. She put it in the pocket of her apron. Her eyes were shiny, but she didn't let them cry.

When Oma left the room with the letter Papa said: "They all died in the concentration camps. Only Fanny is left. She and her husband Clement hid in a farm, but the rest of the family was arrested in Paris before they had a chance to leave."

I remembered the cozy house we used to visit on a quiet street on the outskirts of Paris.

Great-Uncle Shmerl — where are you?

I can still smell the hot pink, blue, green or yellow mixes he used to pour on shiny marble slabs. They quickly dried into a glaze-like icy mix. He took a wooden mallet, carefully breaking it into small pieces. He threw them into huge buckets to be packaged and sold as rock candy. Sometimes, he'd sprinkle nuts onto the slimy surface before it dried. Pretty brown almonds that became shiny, imprisoned in stillness. He moved them around with a long stick, distributing them evenly before the candy dough cooled and dried.

Great-Uncle Shmerl — where are you?

For me, he'd pour a little glob on the corner of the marble slab. He quickly formed it into a doll, with heads, legs and arms stretched out wide.

"Do you want pink or green?" he'd ask. Quickly, he'd sprinkle some yellow to form long happy curls; then, two dots of blue eyes and contrasting colored booties.

"Wait. Wait. Don't touch yet!" he'd say, as my little fingers hungered to snatch the doll. "It's very hot," he'd warn me.

I hardly reached the table as I looked up in awe and wonder. His last touch was a stick inserted in a handy place. Then, he scooped up the doll with a flat metal spatula, loosening its grip from the table, and proudly handed it to me.

Sometimes a woman's voice would call out in the background.

Great-Aunt Sarah, where are you?

"Let's have lunch before you eat the candy," she'd say.

We'd come upstairs from the basement of the house, where the candy factory was located. Their home was pretty. I remember a large black piano on which Aunt Fanny played. Her sister Rachel would admire my doll, saying: "My father has such talent. Too bad his beautiful creations must be eaten!" she'd sigh regretfully.

Aunt Rachel, where are you?
Great-Aunt Sarah, where are you?
Great-Uncle Shmerl, where are you?

Now I hear I will never see you again. Who will make the candies of this world? How could it ever be sweet again?

Aunt Fanny was the only one left. Papa said she told him in the letter that she had two daughters now, Béatrice and Irène.

"Did you hear?" Yvonne said, pushing my arm. "We have new cousins!"

"Will we meet them soon?" I asked Papa.

"Maybe," Papa said, with a faraway look. "But we must stay here now. We must wait. Maybe Maman will find us. Maybe she will come one day."

Yvonne looked at me. Papa didn't know we had read his notebook. We knew the truth.

"Maybe she'll come to look for us," he repeated, as his eyes looked far, far away.

22

AUNTS, UNCLES AND SOME COUSINS TOO

I am going to write to the family," Papa said one day. "I will ask them to visit — the ones that can." We knew what he meant.

The first reply came from *Tante* Méry, as we called our aunt in Toulouse. We knew they had survived. She had been the one to make arrangements with Le Château to take us in after the liberation.

"I will come to see you two Sundays from now," she wrote. "Armand will come with me and so will Henri. Tell me if you need things from the city."

"Oh!" I jumped, letting some happiness lighten my usual sadness. "Armand, Armand. It will be good to see you my dear cousin!" I exclaimed.

We were the same age. His skin was fair. He had blue eyes — quite opposite to my coloring.

"Nenoushou," aunt Méry would call me, using one of my nicknames, when we were on an outing together. "Hold hands and tell everyone he is your brother," she'd say through puckered lips that blew little kisses in the air, savoring the idea he was not an only child.

We had met in Toulouse for the first time in 1940 after we had run from our cozy house near Paris. They had come all the way from Amsterdam where they lived, fleeing the Nazis, hoping they'd be safe here. But that was when France was still free, before the Germans occupied the entire country.

Méry was Maman's first cousin. We had stayed with them for a while before moving to the little village of Grenade, twenty kilometers away. They lived in this small walk-up apartment. She, her husband Henri, and their precious son Armand. It was cramped because extra people always lived there if they had no other place. *Tante* Méry never said no.

The so-called bedroom housed everyone, because the front room was aunt Méry's *atelier*, as she called the living room. A bed for two was shared by three, a bed for one by two, and the rest settled in every corner on the floor, as best as could be provided.

Tante Méry was the most fun person I had ever met. She was a hat maker. The living room was filled with felts, and straws shaped in all kinds of funny ways, bits of ribbon, feathers and beads used to adorn her creations. The ladies came in to try on the hats, and she'd mold and decorate them right on their heads.

"It's exquisite!" she'd exclaim, viewing her creations from every side, her arms outstretched in sheer delight. "Fits you like a dream." And then, "Yes, I'll take one chicken for it — thank you," she'd say, as she was handed the pre-arranged payment for the hat. "And for the straw with the pink ribbon — a dozen eggs will do! Ten? Very well, you look divine!"

When no one cared but for their life, she was still making hats and finding women to buy them. With this she fed the family.

Tante Méry was short, plump, with dark shiny skin that glistened with oiliness. Her black hair frizzled around the round face framing the black eyes that bounced in constant motion. She moved fast on high-heeled shoes she wore to appear taller. Maman's blond hair, blue eyes and slender body were opposite to her. Yet, they were closer than sisters. With all the pain, I would see them giggle like two little girls whenever they were together.

And then we left, and they went into hiding, and we never heard from each other until the war ended.

I couldn't wait to see her. She was a little bit of Maman, with her warm vivacious embraces.

Papa also wrote to Maman's older sister Eva. She, her husband Chil and their daughter Mona had been hiding in a tiny village called Byzanos, all the way down south near the town of Pau. Four years in a cellar, we had heard. Never leaving, never seeing the light. Fed by kindly neighbors who helped them survive. Aunt Eva had come to Le Château after she found out Papa and Maman were gone and we were left alone. "My sister's children are mine now!" she had told Gisèle.

She had taken us to visit them in Byzanos and had wanted to keep us there. But they all lived in one little attic room, hardly surviving, and Gisèle convinced her we were better off at Le Château, at least until later when they got resettled. Who knows where we finally would have ended up? But then, when Papa returned...

Papa soon got an answer from Aunt Eva too. She said yes, they would come to see Papa and us, and help plan the future. She told Papa about people from the family and friends who were missing. She told him about others who had escaped and reappeared.

One of Maman's sister's, Sophie, and one brother, Izzy, had perished. Another, David, had found his way to America on the last boat leaving Europe. He had even managed to take his old parents Jetka and Samuel, along with him, and so they had been saved. Another sister, Thea and her daughter Irène, who was my age, were back in Paris. They had been hiding in some farm in the north.

Papa set a date, and the ones who could come did. It wasn't a happy day because they all cried when they spoke of Maman. All they wanted was for Papa to tell them about the camps, and exactly what happened to Maman.

Even though I had looked forward to the visit I felt sad. Life would never be the same for us. They could not take Maman's place and I realized, more than ever before, that our loss couldn't be replaced. There was only one who really cared, to whom we really belonged, and that one was no more.

Papa looked very troubled about explaining things to them. He said: "Here — what took place is described in these pages. I cannot tell you more. You'll understand," he said, as he handed them the notebook.

The word **TESTIMONY** was etched in large solid letters across the cover. Uncle Henri picked up the book, the blue lines neatly filled the pages.

"I'll start reading it to you," he said to the others, who were sitting around the table in the front room.

Papa left. They sat, eyes opened wide. No one could believe

such things could be. No one did.

Some loose pages, which Yvonne and I had not yet seen, were lying in a separate folder. We went to a corner of the room to look.

(From the writings of my father, done upon his return from camp in 1945, after his liberation.)

THE NEW "HAGGADAH"

It's Pesach eve, the table is set.
Everybody is gay and happy,
The Haggadah was begun before the "gefilte fish,"
And was continued after the meal.

The youngest in the house asked the questions.
Why do we eat today unleaved bread?
Thereupon the father must say:
In memory of our suffering.

We were serfs in the land of the Egyptians
Carrying sand and bricks
Until God with his mighty hand
Brought us to the Red sea shore.

The old stories, they were beautiful.
We loved listening to them.
But now I will write you a new Haggadah
For the old one is by now out of date...

Even though it is closely related to the old one
And also speaks of our suffering.
Yet Moses is quite unknown here

And the background is rather vague.

Here the pyramids are replaced
By monuments of Germanic culture.
Murderers drove us to death from exhaustion
And burned us, leaving no trace.

Here, too, we carried sand and bricks
And our spirits flagged sometimes.
Our wages were cruel beatings
Because we were only a worthless "commodity."

How often did we look up to "Above"
Hoping to see miracles in the sky.
We built the crematories with our own hands
To burn there those who were dearest to us.

Birkenau was the name of that land,
It was a place somewhere in Poland.

Where were you, oh God, with your mighty hand.
To deliver us from there.

Many, so many were sent up to you...
And many, so many took their own lives...
We might have done it, too,
But...Patton did interfere.

Patton and his tank spearheads
Came when despair was greatest,
To him we want to express our thanks,
Because without him we all would be dead.

You should always remember
How hopeless was our world.

No one was there to guide us,
The sentence was passed long before.

How enormous the number of those who remained there.
Of them you should speak throughout eternity,
Of those who floated as clouds of smoke over Birkenau,
The victims of unspeakable crimes.

WHY, DEAR GOD?

Wretched I stand before you, dear God,
I lower my eyes to the ground.
Do answer my questions,
Do look back at your deeds.

Was it really true to your thinking
To have us brought to Birkenau?
Didn't you smell up there
The reek of roasted good things?

Have you really not seen
What was done to your children?
Didn't you see the "crematories"
Where your people were destroyed?

What went on in your thoughts
Or perhaps you preferred not to think?
Millions and millions were killed.
How, dear God, did you guide the world?

It all began with the Jews in Poland.
Only few of them survived.
They were brought in from every country
To end their lives in the ovens.

Men, women, little children,
No one, no one was spared.

Israel was like a herd of cattle
And Adolf Hitler ruled over them!
Have you really never heard of Hitler
Or should I tell you about him?
Did really nothing, nothing at all, disturb you?
Didn't you see the miserable crowds?

And the smoke that rose to heaven?
And you didn't know what it meant?
The war against us was a special war
Not like a war between respectable people.

Your name was bespattered with dirt,
Filthy jokes were told about you.
They laughed about Jehovah, the old God.
What were you thinking then?

Did you think
That we had been bad for a time
And that, therefore, we should suffer...a little.

The days are coming and going
And they are all alike
And there is no end in sight
Of this unbelievable suffering.

I want so much to live,
To know how the end will be.
I have given so much,
I have given so very much.

And if I plead for my life,
It is not for fear of death.
It is to see again
My children, my two precious ones.

And my wife, my beautiful treasure,
What has happened to her I ask?
I yearn for her, I long for her,
Will I ever see her again?

Oh God in heaven, I stand before you,
A poor and penitent sinner,
Grant me one wish, one wish only,
To see again my dear children.

I do admit, we were not good,
Have sometimes forgotten your laws.
But your judgement is not very just either
And is certainly much too severe.

(Original writings in Photo/Document section)

In the folder we did not see the poem Papa wrote: *"It's Annette's Birthday."* Papa did not let them see the poem about Maman. That one was his secret — and ours too now.

Anyway, they were so upset they asked Uncle Henri to stop reading. They couldn't hear anymore.

When they left nothing was resolved. We were alone with our pain. No one could share it. They needed to escape. It was just us. We'd have to find our way — somehow.

23

CAN'T YOU SAY IT ON THE RADIO?

P apa had asked *Tante* Méry to bring a radio from Toulouse. "I must have it," he told her. "Please do not fail to find one and to bring it. We cannot obtain it here."

It was almost like a square brown box with two black knobs on each side, a piece of canvas in the middle. In the center it curved up on top, so it looked a little like the front of a house under a round roof.

The left button gave a click and the radio went on when you turned to the right and off to the left. The right button moved a needle in the center where numbers were printed. Some numbers talked and some played music. Some numbers just made funny giggly noises, so you couldn't hear anything clearly.

Papa put the end of the cord that hung from the back of the radio into the outlet in the front room. You could either use the radio, or the light bulb, not both at the same time. Papa didn't seem to care. At night, we'd use the oil lamp or candles. Papa only wanted to listen to the radio from the moment he got it. "Papa, can we hear some music on the other numbers?" We would ask sometimes.

"No. I must listen to the messages," he would reply sternly, as he sat hours and hours, hearing them sound again and again.

All day long the radio blasted: "Sarah Kahn is looking for her brother Georges, her daughter Mara. Jacques Levi is looking for his wife Sonia, his son Henri. Miriam Ruben is looking for her husband David, her mother Leah. Daniel Abram is looking for his father Vladek, his sister Simone."

It was so strange all these people searching on the radio. Would they ever find each other? Those lost souls on earth?

"Why can't they get together? Aren't they home, or going home, to find their families as you did, Papa?" we asked.

"No. Many don't know where to look. Entire families were scattered. Most died in the camps. The few left don't know how to find each other. They have no homes. No place. It's all in vain," he added sadly. "All in vain," he repeated.

Just the same, he sat near the radio night and day. Sometimes he would jump. "Oh! Jacob made it!" He had recognized a name. Someone he had shared a bunk with, or a piece of bread.

"Sarah Kahn is looking for her brother Georges, her daughter Mara. Jacques Levi is looking for his wife Sonia, his son Henri. Miriam Ruben is looking for her husband David, her mother Leah. Daniel Abram is looking for his father Vladek, his sister Simone."

We really weren't listening to the names anymore, as they kept repeating and repeating like an endless litany.

We had asked Papa once: "Do you think Maman might look for us on the radio?"

"No. No. Maman isn't coming back. You must not sit and wait. There is nothing to wait for. The hell I came from will burn in me to the last day. The fire will never go out. It swallowed her. Don't wait my children. Don't wait."

I missed her. Missed having a mother. But what scared me most is that I was almost forgetting her. She was escaping me. She truly was, and I was frightened.

A person you love has a taste, an aroma, a subtle physical presence that you feel breathing around you. These are the things, more than skin and hair, that are familiar, that are felt. The aura — the aura was gone.

I had tried so many times during those terrible year to feel her scent, remember the warmth of her embrace, recall the melody of her voice. Slowly, subtly, it had eluded me.

My voice could say the words: "*Maman. Petite Mère. Maman.*" But I wasn't sure, anymore, exactly what they meant. How I had longed for her, dreamt, hoped, prayed, implored. "Give her back to me. Please." But my wish had not been granted.

Even though her picture was lovingly placed on the altar during Mass, in a little white envelope, so God would remember to return her to me.

Even though I spoke to her every night before falling asleep.

"Maman, do you hear me? Wherever you are. Remember me? Maman, don't leave me to them. I know you said you sold me the day of the baptism, but you can buy me back, Maman. I'll sin all mortal sins. They'll sell a sinner back to you. Even if my mortal sins condemn me to hell forever, the burning will be later. Now, the burning is slow. It consumes me inside. Only your love could ease it. Maman, they don't need a sinner like me. They'll sell me back to you. Please come. Please come to buy me back."

Even though, Even though, Even though.

Now Papa said she was gone forever, and I could not even recall the exact presence I had longed for incessantly since the day I stood watching the truck leave.

The truck surrounded by the boots, the helmets, the rifles. The truck from which they whispered, "Bye, bye, bye..." accompanied by sad limp hands waving weakly in the air.

"Sarah Kahn is looking for her brother Georges, her daughter Mara. Jacques Levi is looking for his wife Sonia, his son Henri. Miriam Ruben is looking for her husband David, her mother Leah. Daniel Abram is looking for his father Vladek, his sister Simone."

"And I am looking for my Maman.
My Maman has blue eyes.
My Maman has blond hair.
My Maman has fresh pink skin.
My Maman sings prettily.
My Maman likes dresses with flowers all over.
Can't you say it on the radio?
A little girl is looking for her Maman?
She doesn't exactly remember her smell,
the touch of her hands,
the feel of her skin.
But, if she is there, somewhere,
please let her find me.
Because I am her little girl.

And I would like to remember.
And I would like to have her again.
Let me have a new life.
Let me come back to this world,
And have a mother once more."

The days went by, one after the other. We left for school, and Papa sat near the radio. When we came home he was still there. The large notebook was always at his side, the pen resting nearby.

"Sarah Kahn is looking for her brother Georges, her daughter Mara. Jacques Levi is looking for his wife Sonia, his son Henri. Miriam Ruben is looking for her husband David, her mother Leah. Daniel Abram is looking for his father Vladek, his sister Simone."

Papa looked a little more like himself now.

It had been so frightening seeing him right after he had returned from the concentration camp. He had no hair on his head. He was all bones, covered by skin that stretched like the round surface of a drum. He reminded me of a skeleton I had seen in the science books.

"Is that what we look like after we die?" I wondered. I really wasn't sure it was Papa after all. The huge black eyes, shiny, moist, looked bigger in the narrow face.

But, they were his eyes, my eyes, our eyes, and even if they had been transplanted in another body, they were Papa's — Papa's very own — and the rest of the shell would have to grow around them somehow.

With time, and Oma's love and ours, it did, somewhat — but not completely. Something was missing. We knew he would never be the same.

"Maybe we should leave Grenade?" Oma once asked him.

"No. We must stay here," he replied, without giving an explanation.

Papa didn't want to leave Grenade. Was he hoping? Was he waiting? In spite of it all. Could she, or her spirit, come back here? Could she find us? Maybe?

Anyway, where could we go? After Buchenwald and Birkenau Papa no longer cared or longed for anything. He had found us, not really expecting to, and that alone had taken all his strength.

Now we all lived from day to day, listening to the radio.

"Sarah Kahn is looking for her brother Georges, her daughter Mara. Jacques Levi is looking for his wife Sonia, his son Henri. Miriam Ruben is looking for her husband David, her mother Leah. Daniel Abram is looking for his father Vladek, his sister Simone."

24

YOU,
WHO ARE
SEARCHING
FOR ME,
HAVE
WE
LOST
EACH
OTHER
IN THIS
HOLOCAUST?

Sarah Kahn is looking for her brother Georges, her daughter Mara. Jacques Levi is looking for his wife Sonia, his son Henri. Miriam Ruben is looking for her husband David, her mother Leah. Daniel Abram is looking for his father Vladek, his sister Simone. Annette Fersen is looking for her husband Maurice, her daughters Yvonne and Renée."

It was a sunny Sunday morning. Oma had made a big pot of hot *café au lait* and baked some fresh buns all brown outside and sweet-smelling inside.

Our white bowls were full as we slowly dunked broken pieces of the fragrant rolls with the right hand and carefully lifted the left to drink the hot brew.

The liquid spilled over the wooden table as Papa's bowl came down in a crash. The light brown *café au lait* slowly trickled toward the edges in little streams that divided like a river. Then the drops started falling like small stars that lost their way, running to the bench and into our laps.

Such were the words we thought we heard that morning in Grenade, sitting around the wooden table in the front room.

Papa's eyes lost their clarity. They seemed to roll as though he was about to faint. We all stared at him intently and then at each other. Silent thoughts burning our skin traveled like lightning.

Did you hear what I heard? Did I dream?

Are games being played here?

On me? On you? On us? To mock us? To haunt us?

Not a word was uttered by anyone. We all waited for Papa. He would speak. No one else dared. Slowly regaining his composure he said:

"Don't move. I am not sure.

Did you hear it? Did everyone hear it?

They make mistakes, you know.

People have names that sound the same.

They fool you. I heard it a thousand times.

You think you hear — and then it's a mistake!"
He was trembling and very pale. I wasn't sure anymore.
Did they say "Annette," or did they say "Odette"?
Did they say "Maurice," or did they say "Panisse"?
Did they say "Yvonne," or did they say "Dionne"?
Did they say "Renée," or did they say "Aimée"?
Now Papa said: "We must sit. All together, here. Don't move. No one is to move. We shall listen until the night. Until we hear again if they make the same announcement. Then, each of us will listen carefully, to be sure we all heard the same names being called out. We will do nothing until we hear the names again. It's not possible. Don't dream it's possible. Just let's sit here and wait."

It had been many weeks since Papa had returned. Most survivors who knew where to return had done so. They had all been liberated months before.

Yes, people looked for each other because they had all been displaced; but if you knew where to find your family, you would have gone there immediately. That is why Papa knew it could not be Maman, because if she were alive she would have returned to find us long ago.

We sat, waiting and trembling with anticipation — a small glimmer of hope, despite the hopelessness.

Hours and hours passed as we stared, hugging the precious radio, silently praying it would confirm our dream, telling us once more what we wanted to hear, almost sure it had been an hallucination.

As the messages continuously went on we waited, breaths held, eyes glued, afraid to miss a moment. By now the names were like thin threads of memory, vague shapeless echoes, as we had heard their sound repeated over and over on the radio.

What if — Sarah Kahn had found her brother Georges, her daughter Mara, and, Jacques Levi had found his wife Sonia, his son Henri, and Miriam Ruben had found her husband David, her mother Leah, and Daniel Abram had found his father Vladek, his sister Simone, and Maman's name was attached to them, and vanished before we knew if it was really her that was looking for us?

Tiredness and the endless wait stretched our longing. It was late at night. Our uninterrupted vigil was heavy like a blanket.

Then, like a sting, the familiar voice once again came on.

We sat up. Our backs arched, eyes bursting with anticipation. Our hands reached out to each other, needing strength to bear the disappointment we all expected.

"Sarah Kahn is looking for her brother Georges, her daughter Mara. Jacques Levi is looking for his wife Sonia, his son Henri. Miriam Ruben is looking for her husband David, her mother Leah.

Daniel Abram is looking for his father Vladek, his sister Simone.

Annette Fersen is looking for her husband Maurice, her daughters Yvonne and Renée."

"ANNETTE! MAURICE! YVONNE! RENÉE!

Yes, Papa! Yes, Papa!

You heard! I heard!

She heard! We heard!"

Maybe there is another with such names, but they are our names too, so maybe she is ours, and we are who she is looking for!"

We were jubilant, screaming with happiness, tearing the silence of the night, crying and laughing, hugging each other, brushing against salted tears.

Papa suddenly collapsed on the wooden chair. He put his silver head between the long-fingered precious hands, the hands that wrote like music, the hands of poetry and dreams.

Papa sobbed and shook his head from left to right. We stopped being joyous. We waited for him to tell us, as we quietly sat on the floor, hands resting on his knees, slowly deflating like a multi-colored bouncing ball's painful encounter with a rusty nail.

Almost sounding like a broken record, words hardly formed escaped from his mouth as he explained.

Papa was not sure. Papa was afraid. He did not want us to feel happy yet. He knew it couldn't be, couldn't be. Something was wrong, had to be wrong. Why was fate playing more games? Hadn't he already been played with enough?

"Tomorrow I shall go to Toulouse to contact the organization, to find out," he said. "Then, we will know, know what happened with the names, know for sure."

No one dared speak anymore. We all went to bed. This was a long night — heavy with doubt and hope and fear. It's worse when you *almost*, but *not-for-sure* hold a treasure in your hand!

The next day Papa left early, solemnly promising he would return as soon as possible, when he knew the answer.

I had always heard the adults say: "Patience is a virtue!"

I could never understand why patience was such a good thing. I didn't feel that way. To me patience was torture! Why wait for something good? I want to hold it now. Why wait for something bad? I want to walk over it now, destroy it, move on. The long hours of waiting after Papa left that morning were a torture.

Papa returned the next day. He looked confused. He hadn't shaved or changed, and the white stubble of his beard made his black eyes look darker and more sunken under the heavy eyebrows.

"They say it most likely is Maman," he said "but they know nothing definite. It's just her name. It could be someone else. They told me she is very far away in a small village, way up in Sweden. A group of French women had been rescued from the camp by the Red Cross and transported there.

They confirmed she'd been in Auschwitz, in the infamous BLOC 10 where Nazi doctors tortured women by conducting medical experiments under the criminal Doctor Mengele. Most of them were almost dead, or badly damaged, when they were liberated.

They had been transferred to a special rehabilitation center in Sweden to be brought back to life. Apparently, they were too ill to be conscious of what was happening to them, which is why they had not been heard from before. Now, the ones that were saved and survived were starting to look for members of their family that might still be alive.

They cannot be released until it is know that someone can take care of them. Some are maimed forever — others might eventually regain a normal life."

Papa looked very sad, very scared, very happy too.

But, who knew? Who knew if sometimes it was better not to be saved? He had seen the horrors. He had begged for the end many times himself. Which was better? I guess Papa wasn't sure. He knew things we didn't understand.

Papa said he hoped this wasn't another cruel deception. That no one was playing a trick on us.

"Lela told me she had heard from others that Maman had vanished shortly after that death march in the snow from Auschwitz to Ravensbruck, that she had been deathly ill there and had surely not survived. The months that went by without a word were further proof. I hope there is nothing wrong here — nothing wrong," he kept repeating.

Even though there were doubts and unanswered questions, a new dimension had been added to our life now. We waited to be a family again. But first, we had to wait to be reunited with Maman.

What would it be like?

What would *she* be like?

25

CAN WE SURVIVE BEING STRANGERS?

Now that we knew Maman would eventually return, some preparations were made. Maman's clothes were taken out of the boxes where they had been stored, to be aired on a clothes line in the garden.

I went to look and, standing there among the sad dark skirts and jackets, I suddenly saw — I suddenly knew — I suddenly felt — it would be fine.

We had survived.

It would be fine.

It was blowing in the wind, her chiffon scarlet blouse. With its soft pleats running down the front. The shiny mother-of-pearl buttons holding it together. The transparent fabric shimmering with happiness in the sunshine. The sleeves, floating in the wind like butterflies. I had forgotten its existence, but now I remembered it all.

It was her. Her color.

She was waving to me. Smiling.

Flying as fast as she could, to be near and hold me.

I approached the deep pink scarlet chiffon blouse, slowly reaching out to touch the right sleeve, feeling it between my fingers, caressing it gently.

I lifted my left hand to hold on to the other sleeve. And then, I opened my arms wide and hugged her tightly, holding the entire bodice of the blouse and burying my head in the soft pleats in front.

I stayed there for what seemed like an eternity. I had recalled all I had lost.

Maman's blond hair, always so prettily arranged.

Her gentle blue eyes, twinkling with sparks.

Her quick movements, trim but soft.

Her lovely scent.

She was here.

Fully. Completely.

She told me to laugh.

To be happy. To be a child again.

Because soon she would be here,
to be my mother again.

Yes. She told me so, and now the waiting did not matter any more. The blouse had become alive, and I whispered sweet things to it. It was good to be able to talk to Maman again.

Papa went back to Toulouse a number of times to make arrangements to have Maman repatriated, as they called it.

If it was really Maman, he kept saying, not quite believing it was.

If we just got a letter from her. "Some proof!" he insisted. But the people in charge said it was hard to get mail across these days. All they had were names, and if errors were made they couldn't check them out until the people returned. There just wasn't enough organization to get all these displaced persons back where they belonged not to speak of the care that was needed for most of them who where ill and had no one and no place to go back to.

There were a lot of big problems to solve.

PAPERS, PAPERS HAD TO BE OBTAINED.

Yes, I remembered. Papers could decide if you could go to Free France or not. If you had no papers, you had to break through the barricades and get shot at while you drove through. I hoped Maman wouldn't have to do this again.

Please give Maman the papers this time, so she can fill the scarlet blouse which is waiting for her. Don't make Maman drive the car again and be shot. Let her come through. They say she is weak and ill. Please give her the papers. The papers that say she can pass freely, to come home to Free France...

LET HER GO! LET HER GO! Please.

AND THEN, THEY WERE ASKING:

Could we take care of her?
Did we have enough food?

Would she have the medication she needed?
"Yes, we will have the food.
And the medicine. And the love.
And we will make her better.
So much better.

LET HER GO! LET HER GO! Please."

AND THEN, THEY WANTED TO KNOW:

Would we be there to transport her after they brought her from Stockholm to Paris? Would we be there to hold her? To care for her on the trip?

"Yes, we'll be there.
We'll wait at the train station.
We'll hold her hand.
We'll carry her, if needed.
We'll have flowers.
We'll smile.
We'll be happy.

LET HER GO! LET HER GO! Please."

Then one day, came a letter. And, in the letter, was a flower. A dried rose. A pink one. Its crushed petals almost crumbled as we gently lifted it to hold in our trembling hands.

June 4, 1945

My dearest little girls,
I have again the opportunity of sending you a letter which will be taken by air and posted in Paris so it will get there faster. I have already written several times, but have never received a reply.

How are you? I am very worried and think of you night and day. If only I could have a note from you, to see your dear handwriting, to have a photo of you, it would make me so happy. When I arrived in camp at Auschwitz they took the last thing that I had left of you, your photos. They separated me from my beloved Papuschka, poor little Daddy, where could he be?

As long as I will not be reunited with you, and Papi, my suffering will not end. What can life be for us 3 without Papuschka. If only you had sign of life from him and could transmit it to me before they send me home, what joy that would be for me. To travel back to you and at last see you again is something I did not believe could be realized, because we were buried alive.

Now I am already better and you will find again an old little mother who, nevertheless, has kept a young heart to better understand her beloved 2 little girls.

We are here in Sweden, awaiting to be sent back and I hope it will be soon. The country is beautiful and the nature very wild. I swim, walk, and think if only I would have my 2 little ones and Papuschka here how my joy would be fulfilled, but, alas, it is not so.

I am here with 200 comrades of misery, and I live my days with a charming girl who does everything to lift the depression that I always have. I live as a recluse and am anxious to go home.

My dear Yvonne and Renée, I hope you are in good health. Write me what Grandmother is doing, is she in good health? Send the addresses of Madame Coles, Aunt Eva, Aunt Méry.

How are your 2 Godmothers, the Reverend Mother, Father Agathange, Sister Marie-Beatrix. Please transmit the wonderful remembrance that I have of them.

I finish keeping hope that I will receive a small letter from you. While I wait, your little mother kisses you with all her heart.

Annette

PS: Awaiting the pleasure of knowing you I take the liberty of adding a little note to your mother's letter.

A friend,
Gilette

(Original letter in Photo/Document section)

A few days later another letter came.

June 17, 1945

My dear ones,

I have no news from you. It is worse now that I am free not knowing if I shall find you when I return. But you must be there, you must be there.

I've survived because my two best friends in the camp were named Yvonne and Renée. They are with me now. I call out their names frequently. Yvonne. Renée. The sound keeps me alive.

Be there my beloved children. I beg you, be there.

Maman

Then Maman had a separate paper inside the envelope. On top she had scribbled these words: *This is how we were liberated. I thought you would want to know how I came to Sweden.* The handwriting was shaky, not quite clear, but it was Maman. Now we knew. Now we knew for sure.

On April 27, 1945 began our resurrection.

This morning comes the order: All French women are to assemble immediately on the central place. I join them but am sent back because the order refers only to Aryan women. However, there are not enough of them and, in the afternoon, the Jewish French women are also called up.

Sensational rumors are flying through the camp. It seems the Swedish government is getting out several thousand women.

We feel we are going mad. But then, the numbers are removed from our clothing and, lined up in rows of five, we are leaving the camp.

On the outside, we see a great number of marvelous buses. We are invited to get into them, about 30 women in each. We see representatives of the British Red Cross who care for us, and I get a sobbing fit. I can't grasp it. Everything seems too unreal. I tremble and think it is a dream. Am I really free, alive, and will I see my most precious ones.

But it is not a dream. Something none of us believed possible has become reality.

We drive off, we are fed like spoiled children but we cannot swallow anything. We get to Denmark and then by boat to Sweden. For the last two months the Swedes have helped us to recover from our suffering. I cannot put into words what they are doing for us. I shall never forget how devotedly the Swedes took care of us.

(Original letter in Photo/Document section)

Papa said Maman would be released in July. He said it was no use writing because they couldn't forward all the mail people wanted to send. The survivors were constantly moved in different places according to their health, and how they recuperated. Recuperated — what a big word, I thought, for describing how you help my Maman be a person again.

Couldn't you use a smaller word?
A word that would say how she'll be.
How we'll feel when we see her.
Will she smell the same?
Look the same?

26

WILL
WE
EVER
TOUCH
AGAIN?

Finally one day Papa came home and said, "they agreed to let her go." They gave Papa a date. They said we should get ready for that day.

Papa told us he would leave the night before, to be sure he was on time. He would take the train to Toulouse, one hour away, and then the big train to Paris, seven hours away.

He would bring Maman back the next day. Papa said he couldn't take us because it might be too much emotion for Maman to see us all at once. First, she would see him, and slowly get ready to meet us again. Papa knew what was best. We would wait here for them. Maybe he wanted to see first? Maybe Papa wasn't sure about something.

And soon, the day came. The house was scrubbed and cleaned.

We prepared nice food. We baked. We filled vases. The flowers were smiling from every corner.

It was early in the morning.

The summer sun winked at us through the open windows.

The white lace curtains whispered joyously.

We wore our best.

We wanted to make a good impression.

This was the day!

JULY 7, 1945

WELCOME HOME! MAMAN.

We had drawn the sign on a large piece of cardboard with multi-colored crayons. We had pasted things on it — little pieces of grass, tiny branches, fuzzy feathers, bits of flowers — to make it more decorative.

The sign was dancing, right there on top of the blackened

hearth, in the front room, Papa and Maman's room.

We were pacing, nervously arranging this and that all around, as though it really mattered, as though Maman would care.

Yvonne looked at the sign. "Did you notice the date?" she remarked. "*July 7, 1945.* It was *July 7, 1943* they were deported from here. Remember?"

Two years. Two years to the day. To the hour. Maybe to the minute. How strange. Did God count the time? Did he say:

"You shall be held in bondage for two years. And then you shall be freed."

Was there a reason? Why did they take two years from her life? *Why?*

I glanced at Yvonne. I wouldn't have made it without her. She had been my mother all that time. I noticed how anxious she was, suddenly realizing that, in a way, she was losing her place. She would be a child with a mother now — no longer mother of a child. She was all grown up. Just turned sixteen. Would she know what her new place would be? Would she know how to behave? How to obey? Follow directions? She, who had taken charge so completely.

I came close to her and took her hand, slightly squeezing our fingers together. She looked at me strangely.

Oh my God! I thought, feeling a shiver engulf my body. Maybe she doesn't really want Maman back. Maybe she wants to keep her place. She is the mother now.

"I love you," I said, looking up, trying to tell her. To let her know I would always be hers, no matter what. Let her know she'd never lose me — ever.

"I know," she replied in a shaky voice. "So do I love you. Very much. I hope things work out, that everything will be all right," she added, with some apprehension.

Soon there was a knock on the door. The pounding inside my chest was so loud it echoed through my head, making me feel dizzy.

Oma rushed to open it.

Papa entered first and turned extending his hand to the woman, gently pulling her inside the hall and into the front room.

"Come in," he said softly.

We stood stiffly facing each other at opposite sides of the room.

Her hair was brown.

She wore pants.

I had never seen a woman in pants.

Around her waist was a belt that closed in front,

with some little trinket that looked like a tiny sword.

Was she ours? Were we hers?

We looked at each other, almost with suspicion.

She called out our names.

YVONNE? RENÉE?

YVONNE? RENÉE?

I didn't know the voice.

She searched into our eyes. Deep, deep inside. Turning her head from side to side. From one to the other. We stood, frozen at attention.

"THEY ARE NOT MINE!" she screamed at Papa.

"THESE ARE NOT MY CHILDREN!

My children are dead.

I knew you didn't tell me the truth.

You didn't bring them to the station,

because they are not mine.

I knew you lied. It's all over.

Why did I live? It's all over now."

Papa tried to calm her down. He explained he had not brought us to the station because he wanted to spare her too great a shock. He kept repeating.

"Please, believe me," he begged, now realizing it had been an error of judgement to leave us behind.

Turning to us he mumbled how Maman, when she had seen him standing alone at the train station in Paris, had not believed we were alive. She had wanted to jump off the train. She didn't want to live with dead children, she had said. She had only survived to be with us. Now it was all over. She didn't want to

live anymore. Papa had not been able to convince her, and had
great difficulty completing the journey and containing her
hysteria.

And now —

I too knew she was right.

This was *not* my mother.

And I was *not* her child.

She was right.

All I had left now was the empty scarlet blouse. Not a real
flesh and blood mother.

"They are OURS!" Papa screamed, shaking Maman by the
shoulders, in a desperate effort to convince her.

Then, like an animal who jumps on her prey, she grabbed me
and started to rip the clothes off my body.

"I know the marks. I won't be fooled," she screamed in a
strange new voice I did not recognize.

She twisted and turned me until she located the special brown
beauty mark I had always had on my backside. My sister had
one right inside her neck. There were other signs — secret ones
— only she knew, she who had borne us.

Maman was on her knees now.

Her sobs were like the wailing cry of a jungle animal, as she
pawed us with her bare fingers, screaming:

"THEY ARE MINE,
THEY ARE MINE."

Where are you?
YOU
who is searching
for
ME.

WILL WE EVER TOUCH AGAIN?

YOU
now who found
ME.
Will we survive
being strangers?

WILL WE EVER TOUCH AGAIN?

Am I still
your child?
Are you still
my mother?

WILL WE EVER TOUCH AGAIN?

Or
have we lost
each other
in this holocaust?

WILL WE EVER TOUCH AGAIN?

EPILOGUE

Are you wondering,
you who have shared this journey,
what has happened to us all?
Now that we survived.

Did our spirits regain full clarity?
Did our scars heal?
Disappear?

Alas, No.
For even though we went through the motions,
much had to be resolved.

A future, heavy with memories,
too painful to forget.
A return to the truth.
Who were we? Really?
Would we ever understand
the losses,
the insanity of it all?
Could we recapture life?

Papa and Maman kept their promise to the church. We remained fervent Catholics for a long time. They did not interfere. Slowly, we found our way back. But never completely. The thread had been broken and it could never mend.

Soon after Maman's return we left Grenade. Each corner was a reminder of the plague that befell us here. We lived in Toulouse for a while, and eventually returned north to Paris.

Was the sky forever blue, and the sun shining bright for us, you may ask? Now that it was all over...

In some ways yes, in some ways no.

I forever lived in fear of losing Papa and Maman again. When Maman first returned, I followed her every step for months — waiting at the bathroom door, sleeping at the foot of her bed like a frightened sparrow, never for one single moment leaving her side, lest they should take her again.

Yvonne continued to waiver as to who she truly was. What side did she belong to? She had grown up before her time. Was she still an adolescent? Was she already an adult? Where was her place?

Europe had become sad, too filled with memories for Papa and Maman. They needed new horizons, places where they could forget, start anew. In 1949, Yvonne was married in Paris to an American. She moved to New York. Papa, Maman, Oma and I followed later.

Oma lived to hold her first great-grandchild Lynda, Yvonne's first child, born in 1950. A son, David, was born four years later. Oma died in New York, in February of 1953. She was 79 years old.

Papa's nights and days were filled with the horror of what had happened. It is to our ears, and all those who would listen, that he poured out his sorrow. He suffered from the tragedy of the Holocaust until the last days of his life. He died in New York on February 7,1982. He was 79 years old.

Maman refused to dwell on the past. She so much wanted to move on to the future and leave behind the pain, the tortures, inflicted upon her. It is with great courage and spirit that she carefully assembled the fabric of our fragile lives to make it somewhat whole again — as though nothing had happened — as though we could ever forget.

I married in 1958. My husband Bernard was born and brought up in Transylvania, on the border of Romania and Hungary. At the end of the war he was recruited by the Palmach at age sixteen.

Shortly thereafter he left Europe for Palestine, where he enlisted in the Israeli Commandos and fought in the 1948 War of Independance. He then joined the Israeli Navy, as an officer, where he remained for a number of years.

Our son Marc was born in New York in 1962, our daughter Caren in 1964. They are the future, and this story is my offering to them.